The Chapter Of Accidents: A Comedy In Five Acts

Sophia Lee

THE

Chapter of Accidents:

A

C O M E D Y,

IN

F'I V E   A C T S,

As it is performed at all the

T H E A T R E S - R O Y A L

I N

L O N D O N.

WRITTEN by MISS LEE.

THE FOURTH EDITION.

LONDON:
Printed for T. CADELL, in the Strand.
M DCC LXXXII.

PREFACE.

THE averſion a woman ought to feel at the neceſſity of engaging even in a literary conteſt, has induced me to endure a variety of imputations; yet, to publiſh a piece, and leave all unanſwered, might at once give a ſanction to the paſt, and encourage future ſlanders :—— let this plead my excuſe for introducing myſelf to thoſe who have ſo generouſly received a comedy I could wiſh more worthy their patronage.

Charged early in life with the care of a family, I accompanied my father eight years ago in the rules of a priſon, where the perjury of an enemy and the injuſtice of a judge for a time confined him. To amuſe ſome of my melancholy leiſure, I there (from a fondneſs for Marmontel's beautiful tale of Lauretta) firſt conceived a deſign of introducing into the Drama a female heart, capable of frailty, yet ſhuddering at vice, and perhaps ſufficiently puniſhed in her own feelings. A lover, whoſe error was likewiſe in his heart, not head; and even for him I contrived a chaſtiſement in the agony of loſing her: nor did I imagine, in adopting a religious tenet, I could ever be accuſed of offending morality. Subſequent characters and incidents aroſe in the manner they now appear, except that the governor had then no place in it. It is now ſeven years ſince the piece was brought thus forward; ſoon after which a friend lent me a tranſlation of Monſieur Diderot's Pere de Famille,——This fine performance gave me infinite pleaſure under all the diſadvantages of a tranſlation: and the chance-ſimilitude which now and then occurred between that and mine rather flattered

A   than

than grieved me, fince, confcious of my own originality, and imagining even my worft enemy, if he charged me with plagiarifm, would at leaft allow, while the fubject was new to our ftage, my only crime was in denying it.——I returned the tranflated play, and mine lay dormant feveral years. Sentiment was now exploded, and I therefore fought to diverfify it with humour. The character of the auftere Commander in Monfieur Diderot's play had particularly pleafed me; and not being miftrefs of the French language, I fought in vain for a tranflation, on purpofe to interweave him into mine. Not able to meet with any, I created the character of Governor Harcourt, (whofe chief likenefs to the French uncle is in name) and heightened the piece with every event relative to him: but an unbounded partiality I muft ever retain for mufic made me finifh it as a three act opera.

In the interim my father had been engaged as a capital Actor by Mr. Harris. Life opened gradually upon me, and diffipated the illufions of imagination. I learnt that merit merely is a very infufficient recommendation to managers in general! and as I had neither a proftituted pen or perfon to offer Mr. Harris, I gave up, without a trial, all thoughts of the Drama, and fought an humble home in Bath, refolving to bury in my own heart its little talent, and be a poor any thing rather than a poor author. Some valuable friends, I had long poffeffed there, infifted I fhould be wanting to myfelf in configning this piece voluntarily to oblivion, and offered me a recommendation to Mr. Harris, with a promife of concealing my name, unlefs it was accepted. I could defire nothing more: and under thefe circumftances it was put into that gentleman's hands above a twelvemonth ago. The praifes he gave it induced my friend to own my name, and from that moment (let his

confcience

confcience tell him why) it funk in Mr. Harris's favour.
He faid he had frequently refufed a play of Mr. Macklin's
taken from le Pere de Famille, and could not accept another on the fame fubject; infifted that the ferious part of
mine was all Diderot's; advifed me to cut it entirely out,
and convert the humorous part into an after-piece, which
he would bring out in the courfe of the feafon. Reafons
very remote from the Stage could alone induce me to liften.
a moment to his propofal, and thofe brought me a hundred
miles to converfe with him on the fubject; when he produced me the copy fent him, fo worn out and dirty, that
I had reafon to conclude he had lent it to every one he
knew, at leaft.——I was enough miftrefs of myfelf to
liften with complaifance to the moft fupercilious and un-
meaning criticifms, and agreed to mutilate it according to
his ideas. The Actors were now named; I had every reafon to imagine it a fettled thing; and returning to Bath,
fent the reduced copy at the appointed time, viz. early in
September. A month elapfed without my even knowing
he had received it; when, with the continued ill manners
of addreffing me by a third perfon, (for he never wrote a
fingle line in anfwer to feveral letters) I was fhewn a para-
graph from Mr. Harris by the friend already mentioned,
importing, that I " had fent him *four* acts inftead of *two*,
and muft ftill take away half; adding, that he advifed me
by all means to retain my own, difregarding Diderot."
I did retain my own; for as the manufcript was quickly
returned for another alteration, I thought it time to confider what was due to myfelf, and that the character of
mildnefs and complacency would be rather dearly bought
if I gave up all merit for it; I therefore wrote him a civil
letter, and finally withdrew it.

A 2   I fhall

I fhall not expatiate on this treatment. I was perhaps
in fome degree blameable, for believing that man would
fet any value on my time or my money, who knew not the
value of his own; nay, I may be in reality obliged to him
in one fenfe, fince his acceptance of my Comedy would
inevitably have configned to oblivion thofe parts of it ho-
nored with the moft lavifh applaufe.

What pleafure do I feel in retracting the general afper-
fion caft upon managers, when I fpeak of Mr. Colman!—
Obliged to get the piece reprefented if poffible, left the
fubject fhould be borrowed (an evil too common of late) I
enclofed with it an anonymous letter to that Gentleman,
briefly relating thefe particulars, and it was left at his houfe
early in the year by an unknown perfon. At the expira-
tion of a fortnight the manufcript or his anfwer was de-
manded, and the latter by this means rendered both im-
partial and decifive. Mr. Colman thought the general
name of Author entitled to the compliment of his own
hand-writing; and, by a flattering opinion, and immediate acceptance of my piece, encouraged me to avow myfelf. By his advice I cut out the fongs, and lengthened it
into five acts. Nor did his kindnefs end there. He gave
me the benefit of his judgment and experience, both in
heightening and abbreviating the bufinefs, with every at-
tention in cafting and getting it up; generoufly uniting to
the name of Manager that of Friend, Mr. Colman has
brought into notice a woman who will ever with pride and
pleafure acknowledge the obligation.

PROLOGUE.

Written by GEORGE COLMAN, *Esq.*

Spoken by Mr. PALMER.

LONG has the paſſive ſtage, howe'er abſurd,
Been rul'd by *names*, and govern'd by a *word*.
Some poor *cant term*, like magic ſpells can awe,
And bind our realms, like a dramatic law.
When Fielding, Humour's fav'rite child, appear'd,
Low was the word—a word each author fear'd!
'Till chac'd at length, by pleaſantry's bright ray,
Nature and mirth reſum'd their legal ſway ;
And Goldſmith's genius baſk'd in open day.

    No beggar, howe'er poor, a cur can lack ;
Poor bards, of critic curs can keep a *pack*.
One yelper ſilenc'd, twenty barkers riſe,
And with new *howls*, their *ſnarlings* ſtill diſguiſe.
Low baniſh'd, the word *ſentiment* ſucceeds ;
And at that ſhrine the modern playwright bleeds.
Hard fate ! but let each wou'd-be critic know,
That *ſentiments* from genuine *feelings* flow,
Critics in vain diſclaim, and write, and rail :
Nature, eternal Nature ! will prevail.
Give me the bard, who makes me laugh and cry,
Diverts and moves, and all, I ſcarce know why !
Untaught by commentators, French and Dutch,
Paſſion ſtill anſwers to th' electric touch.
Reaſon, like Falſtaff, claims, when all is done,
The honors of the field already won.

To.

To-night, our author's is a mix'd intent—
Paſſion and humour—*low* and *ſentiment :*
Smiling in tears—a ſerio-comic play—
Sunſhine and ſhow'r—a kind of April-Day!
A Lord, whoſe pride is in his honor plac'd;
A governor with av'rice not diſgrac'd;
An humble prieſt! a lady, and a lover,
So full of virtue, *ſome of it runs over.*
No temporary touches, no alluſions
To camps, reviews, and all our late confuſions;
No perſonal reflections, no ſharp ſatire,
But a mere chapter from the book of Nature.
Wrote by a woman too! the muſes now
Few liberties to naughty men allow;
But like old maids on earth, reſolv'd to vex,
With cruel coyneſs treat the other ſex.

P E R-

PERSONS.

Lord Glenmore, - - - - Mr. BENSLEY.

Governor Harcourt, - - - Mr. WILSON,

Woodville, only Son to }
    my Lord, - - - } - Mr. PALMER,

Captain Harcourt, Ne- }
    phew to both, - } - Mr. BANNISTER, Jun.

Grey, an infirm Clergyman, Mr. AICKIN.

Vane, Valet to Lord Glenmore, Mr. LA MASH,

Jacob, Servant to Cecilia, - Mr. EDWIN.

Cecilia, Miftrefs to Woodville, Mifs FARREN,

Mifs Mortimer, Ward to }
    Lord Glenmore, - } - Mrs. CUYLER.

Warner, Houfekeeper to }
    Lord Glenmore, - } - Mrs. LOVE,

Bridget, Maid to Cecilia, - Mrs. WILSON,

Scene, London,

Time, twenty-four Hours

T H

THE
CHAPTER of ACCIDENTS:
A
COMEDY.

SCENE I. *A Hall.*

Enter Vane *in a Riding Drefs, and a Footman.*

Vane. R U N, and tell Mrs. Warner, my Lord is at hand ; and bid the butler fend me a bottle of hock. *(Throws himfelf along the hall chairs, wiping his forehead)* Phew! the months have jumbled out of their places, and we have July in September.

Enter Mrs. Warner,

War. Servant, Mr. Vane.

Vane. Ah, my dear creature! how have you done thefe fifty ages?

War. Why, methinks you are grown mighty grand, or you would have come to the ftill-room to afk; will you chufe any chocolate?

Vane. Why don't you fee I am dead?---abfolutely dead; and, if you was to touch me, I fhould fhake to meer duft, like an Egyptian mummy. Becaufe it was not provoking enough to lounge away a whole fummer in the country, here am I driven up to town, as if the devil was at my heels in the fhape of our hopeful heir; who has neither fuffered my Lord nor me to reft one moment, through his confounded impatience to fee his uncle.

War. Umph,---he'll have enough of the old gentleman prefently. He is the very moral of my poor dear lady, his fifter, who never was at peace herfelf, nor fuffered any one elfe to be fo. Such a houfe as we have had ever fince he came!---why he is more full of importance and airs than a bailiff in poffeffion; and hectors over Mifs Mortimer, 'till fhe almoft keeps her chamber to avoid him.

Vane. Hates Mifs Mortimer!---why, here 'll be the devil to pay about her, I fuppofe?

War. Hate her? ay, that he does. He look'd as if he could have kill'd her, the moment fhe came down to fee him; and got into his chamber prefently after, where he fends for me.---" Who is this young woman, Mrs. What's your name?" fays he. Why, fir, fays I, fhe is the orphan of a Colonel Mortimer, whofe intimacy with my Lord, fays I---" Pho, pho, fays he, all that I know, woman; what does fhe do in this houfe?" fays he; his face wrinkling all over, like fike cream, when it's fkimming. Why, fir, fays I, her father unluckily died, juft before the Duke his brother, and fo could not leave her one fhilling of all that fine fortune; fo my Lord intends to marry her to Mr. Woodville, fays I.——" He does ? cries he; heav'n be prais'd I'm come in time to mar that dainty projeét, however. You may go, woman, and tell Mifs, I don't want any thing more to-night."——So up goes I to Mifs Mortimer, and tells her all this. Lord! how glad fhe was, to find he intended to break the match, though fhe can't guefs what he means.

Vane. Upon my foul, I think it is full as hard to guefs what fhe means. What the devil, will not my Lord's title, fortune, and only fon, be a great catch for a girl without a friend or a fhilling?

War. Ay; but I could tell you a little ftory, would explain all.——You muft know——*(fitting down; a loud knocking.)*

Vane. *(ftarts up.)* Zounds, here's my Lord! [*Exeunt confufedly.*

SCENE, *An Antichamber.*

Lord Glenmore *and the* Governor *meet; the latter hobbling.*

L. Glen. You are welcome to England, brother! I am forry your native air pays you fo ill a compliment after fixteen years abfence.

Gov. Faith, my Lord, and fo am I too, I promife you: I put up with thefe things tolerably well in the Indies; I did not go there to be happy; but,

after

after all my labours, to find I have juft got the money when it is out of my power to enjoy it, is a curfed ftroke:---like a fine fhip of war, I am only come home to be difmafted and converted into an hofpital. However, I am glad *you* hold it better : I don't think you look'd as well when we parted. My fifter, poor Sufan! fhe is gone.too :---well, we can never live a day the longer for thinking on't, Where's Frank ? is he ftill the image of his mother?

L. Glen. Juft as you left him, but that the innocence of the boy is dignified by the knowledge of the man.

Gov. He will hardly remember his old uncle !——— I did love the rogue, that's the truth on't; and never look'd at my money-bags but I thought of him. However, you have provided him a wife ?

L. Glen. I have; you faw her on your arrival, I fuppofe, for I left her in town to attend a fick aunt. Poor Mortimer ! he died one month before the Duke his brother, and miffed a fine title and eftate. You know how I loved the honeft fellow, and cannot wonder I took home his orphan'd daughter, as a match for Woodville.

Gov. Brother, brother, you are too generous; it is your foible, and artful people know how to convert it to their own advantagè.

L. Glen. It is, if a foible, the nobleft incident to humanity. Sophia has birth, merit, accomplifhments; and wants nothing but money to qualify her for any rank.

Gov.

Gov. Can she have a worse want on earth? Birth, merit, accomplishments, are the very things that render money more essential: if she had been brought up in a decent plain way indeed,---but she has the airs of a peeress already; and, if any philosopher doubts of the perpetual motion, I would advise him to watch the knocker of your house. Then you have, out of your precise decorums, removed your son, to make way for this flirt of fashion; and what is the consequence of rendering him thus early his own master?

L. Glen. If you run on thus, only to divert yourself, with all my heart; but, if you would throw a real imputation on Miss Mortimer's conduct, she is entitled to my serious defence. I never saw any good arise from secluding young people; and authorise Woodville and Sophia to live with that innocent elegance, which renders every rank easy, and prevents pleasure from seducing the heart, or ignorance the senses.

Gov. My Lord, I am amazed at you! was there ever yet a woman who didn't mean to pass for a goddess? Do they not gain upon us continually, 'till nothing of our prerogative remains but the name? We are wise fellows truly, if we do not keep down this humour of theirs as long as possible, by breeding them in retirement. Every tinsel fop will find address enough to convince a wife she is an angel; and the husband must be lucky, as well as sensible, who reconciles her to treatment so inferior to her deserts. Woodville will agree with me, I dare say; for the character suits with his intended; and, 'faith, he will

make

make but a modifh hufband, or he could not endure to
fee her flying about, like the queen-bee with the whole
hive at her heels.

L. Glen.   You are too captious, brother!

Gov.   And you too placid, brother! If, like me,
you had been toiling a third of your days to compafs a
favourite defign, and found it difappointed at the moment you thought it complete, what would even your
ferene Lordfhip fay and do?---here have I promifed myfelf a fon in your's,---an heir in your's;---inftead of
which---

L. Glen.   His marriage with Mifs Mortimer will
not make him unworthy either title.

Gov.   Never mention her name to me, I beg, my
Lord!---I hate all mode-mongers of either fex: the
wife, I would 'have given him, has beauty without
knowing it, innocence without knowing it, becaufe
fhe knows nothing elfe, and to furprize you further,
forty thoufand pounds without knowing it---nay, to
bring all your furprizes together, is my daughter without knowing it.

L. Glen.   Your daughter? why have you married
fince my fifter's death? your daughter by *her*, you loft
before you went abroad.

Gov.   Yes, but I fhall find her again, I believe.---
I know you will call this one of my odd whims as ufual,
but we have all fome; witnefs this dainty project of
your's; and fo I will tell you the truth in fpite of that
project---from the very birth of this girl, I faw her mother would fpoil her, and, had fhe lived, propofed kid-
napping Mifs in her infancy.

L. Glen.

L. Glen. Kidnap your own daughter!---why brother I need only prove this to obtain a commiffion of lunacy, and fhut you up for life.

Gov. Why, though my wife was your Lordfhip's fifter, I will venture to tell you fhe was plaguy fantaftical, and contrived to torment me as much with her *virtues,* as others by their *vices*---fuch a fufs about her *delicacy,* her *fenfibility,* and her *refinement,* that I could neither look, move, nor fpeak, without offending one or the other; and execrated the inventor of the jargon every hour in the four and twenty: a jargon, I refolved my girl fhould never learn; and heav'n no fooner took her mother, (heav'n be prais'd for all things!) than I difpatched her draggle-tailed French governefs; made a bonfire of every book on education; whip'd Mifs into a poft-chaife (under a pretence of placing her in a nunnery) inftead of which, I journeyed into Wales, and left her in the care of a poor curate's wife, whofe name was up as the beft houfewife in the whole country; then return'd, with a folemn hiftory of her death in the fmall-pox.

L. Glen. Well, this is indeed aftonifhing! an admirable tutorefs truly for my niece!

Gov. Yes, but there's a better jeft than that.

L. Glen. Indeed!---is that poffible?

Gov. How do you think I contrived to make them obey my inftructions? I faw they fufpected I was fome rich humourift, and was afraid they would, after all, make a little bit of a gentlewoman of her, for which reafon, except the firft year in advance, they never had a fingle fhilling of my money.

L. Glen.

L. Glen. This is almost incredible! and so you left your only child to the charity of strangers?

Gov. No, no, not so bad as that neither.---You remember my honest servant Hardy? after the poor fellow's leg was shot off in my tent, I promis'd him a maintenance; so entrusting him with the secret, I order'd him to live in the neighbourhood, have an eye on the girl, and claim her if ill-used:---fine accounts I had from him, 'faith! the old parson and his wife, having no children, and not finding any one own her, gave out she was *theirs,* and doated on her; in short, she is the little wonder of the country; tall as the palm-tree! with cheeks, that might shame the drawing-room; and eyes, will dim the diamonds I have brought over to adorn them——This confounded gout has kept me in continual alarm, or else she should have spoke for herself.

L. Glen. Why then does not Hardy bring her up to you?·

Gov. Why for two very sufficient reasons:---in the first place, that identical parson paid him the last compliment, that. is, buried him a twelvemonth ago; and in the second, they would hardly entrust her to any man but him who deliver'd her to them.---Here was a girl, my Lord, to support your title, of which I dare swear you are as fond as ever: she would have brought you a race of true Britons; instead of which, from the painted dolls and unjointed Macaronies of these days, we shall produce our own enemies, and have a race of Frenchmen born in England.

L. Glen.

L. Glen. I thank your *intention*, brother; but am far from wiſhing the chief accompliſhments of Woodville's Lady ſhould be the making *cream cheeſes, goats whey,* and *alder wine.*

Gov. Let me tell your Lordſhip, women were never better than when thoſe *were* their chief accompliſhments.——But I may be ridiculous my own way, without being ſingular.——*Harcourt* ſhall have my girl, and my money too.——Cream cheeſes, quotha? no, no, making cream *faces* is an accompliſhment which the belles of theſe days oftener excel in.

L. Glen. I would not adviſe you to publiſh this opinion, Governor!

Gov. But where is this ſon of your's? ſure he has not totally forgot his old uncle?

L. Glen. He will be here immediately.

Gov. Nay, I muſt e'en take an old man's fate, and follow his miſtreſs without complaint.

L. Glen. You have no reaſon for the reproach; this is not his hour for viſiting Miſs Mortimer.

Gov. Miſs Mortimer!—ha, ha, ha! why, do you think I took *her* for his miſtreſs?—what, I warrant, I can tell you news of your own family, though I have hardly been three days in it?——Woodville keeps a girl, and in great ſplendor!—nay, they tell me, that the unconſcionable young rogue encroaches ſo far on the privileges of threeſcore, as to intend marrying the ſlut.

L. Glen. You jeſt ſurely?

Gov. There's no jeſt like a true one——ha, ha, ha! how fooliſh you look!—this is your *innocent elegance,*

C   this

this is the bleſſed effect of letting him live out of your
own houſe!——

L. Glen. Pr'ythee reſerve your raillery, ſir, for
ſome leſs intereſting occaſion ;—to have my views
thus in a moment overturned !——where does ſhe
live?

Gov. Ha, ha, ha!——oh, the difference of thoſe
little ſyllables *me* and *thee !* now you can gueſs what
made me ſo peeviſh, I ſuppoſe?——as to where Miſs
lives, I have not heard ; but ſomewhere near *his*
lodgings.——A deviliſh fine girl ſhe is, by the bye.——
Ah, I told you, twenty years ago, you would ſpoil
this boy,—entirely ſpoil him.

L. Glen. Zounds ! Governor, you have a temper
Socrates himſelf could not have ſupported ;——is this
a time for old ſayings of twenty years ago?——finiſh
dreſſing ;—by that time your nephew will be here, and
I ſhall have reflected on this matter.

Gov. With all my heart,—'tis but a boyiſh frolick,
and ſo good morning to you.——Here ; where's my
triumvirate? Pompey, Anthony, Cæſar? [*Exit.*

L. Glen. A boyiſh frolick truly !——many a fooliſh
fellow's life has been mark'd by ſuch a boyiſh frolick !
——but her reſidence is the firſt object of my enquiry.
——Vane.

Enter Vane.

Is not my ſon come ?

Vane. This moment, my Lord ; and walks 'till the
Governor is ready.

L. Glen.

L. Glen. Vane!——I have deferved you fhould be attached to me, and I hope you are?

Vane. My Lord! (what the devil is he at?) [*Afide.*

L. Glen. This ftrange old Governor has alarmed me a good deal;—you are more likely to know, whether with reafon, than I can be.——Have you heard any thing important of my fon lately?

Vane. Never, my Lord.

L. Glen. Not that he keeps a miftrefs?——what does the fool fmile at?

Vane. I did not think that any thing important, my Lord.

L. Glen. I do, fir---and am told a *more* important thing; that he even thinks of marrying her:---now, though I cannot credit this, I would chufe to know what kind of creature fhe is. Could not you affume a clownifh difguife, and, fcraping an acquaintance with her people, learn fomething of her character and defigns?

Vane. Doubtlefs, to oblige your Lordfhip, *I could* do fuch a thing.——But, if Mr. Woodville's fharp eyes (and love will render them ftill fharper) fhould difcover me, I might chance to get a good drubbing in the character of a fpy.

L. Glen. Oh, it is very improbable he fhould fufpect you:——at the worft, name your employer, and your bones are fafe.——The office perhaps is not very agreeable, but I impofe few fuch on you: execute it well, and you fhall remember it with pleafure.——I will detain Woodville 'till you are ready; and, as I doubt not that his next vifit will be to this

C 2   creature;

creature; by following him you will find out where she lives. Prepare then as quick as possible, and send me word when you are ready; for, 'till then, I will not suffer him to depart.   [*Exit.*

Vane. A pretty errand this his formal Lordship has honor'd me with!——um; if I *betray* him, shall I not get more by it?——ay, but our heir is such a sentimental spark, that, when his turn was served, he might betray *me*. Were he one of our hare-um skare-um, good-natured, good-for-nothing fellows, it would go against my conscience to do him an ill turn.——I believe I stand well in my Lord's will, if Counsellor Puzzle may be trusted, (and, when he can get nothing by a lye, perhaps he may tell truth) so, like all thriving men, I will be honest because it best serves my interest.   [*Exit.*

SCENE, *A Confin'd Garden.*

Woodville *walking about.*

Wood. How tedious is this uncle!——how tedious every body!——was it not enough to spend two detestable months from my love, merely to preserve the secret, but I must be tantalized with seeing without arriving at her? yet how, when I do see her, shall I appease that affecting pride of a noble heart conscious too late of its own inestimable value?——why was I not uniformly just?——I had then spared myself the bitterest of regrets.

Enter

Enter Captain Harcourt.

Har. Woodville ! how do'ſt ?——don't you, in happy retirement, pity me my Ealing and Acton marches and. countermarches, as Foote has it ?——but, methinks thy face is thinner and longer, than a for-ſaken nymph's who is going through the whole ceremony of a nine month's repentance.——What, thou'ſt fall'n in love ?——ruſtically too ?——nay, prithee don't look ſo very lamentable !

Wood. Ridiculous !——keep this Park-converſation for military puppies !——how can we have an eye or ear for pleaſure, when our fate hangs over us unde-cided ?

Har. I gueſs what you mean : but why make mountains of mole-hills ? Is the roſy-fiſted damſel ſo obſtinately virtuous ?

Wood. Imagine a fair favourite of Phœbus in all reſpects ; ſince, while her face caught his beams, her heart felt his genius !—Imagine all the graces hid under a ſtraw hat, and ruſſet gown : imagine——

Har. You have *imagined* enough of conſcience ! and now for a few plain facts, if you pleaſe.

Wood. To ſuch a lovely country maid I loſt my heart laſt ſummer ; and ſoon began to think romances the only true hiſtories ; all the toilſome glories recorded by Livy, phantoms of pleaſure, compared with the mild enjoyments deſcribed by Sir Philip Sydney ; and happineſs not merely poſſible in a cottage, but *only* poſſible there.

Har.

Har. Well; all the philofophers (ancient and modern) would never be able to convince me, a coach was not a mighty pretty vehicle; and the laffes as good-natured in town as country : but pray let us know, why you laid afide the paftoral project of eating fat bacon and exercifing a crook all day, that thou might'ft conclude the evening with the fuperlative indulgence of a peat-fire and a bed ftuff'd with ftraw ?

Wood. Why, faith, by perfuading the dear girl to fhare mine.

Har. Oh, now you talk the language of the world : and does that occafion thee fuch a melancholy face ?

Wood. How ignorant are you both of me and her !——ev'ry moment fince I prevail'd, has only ferv'd to convince me I can fooner live without ev'ry thing elfe than her; and this fatal leifure (caus'd by my abfence with my father) fhe has employ'd in adding ev'ry grace of art to thofe of nature; 'till, thoroughly fhock'd at her fituation, her letters are as full of grief as love, and I dread to hear ev'ry hour I have loft her.

Har. I dread much more to hear you have loft yourfelf. Ah, my dear Woodville, the moft dangerous charm of love is, ev'ry man conceits no other ever found out his method of loving : but, take my word for it, your Dolly may be brought back to a milk-maid. —Leave her to herfelf awhile, and fhe'll drop the celeftials, I dare fwear.

Wood.

Wood. She is too noble : and, nothing, but the duty I owe to fo indulgent a father, prevents me from off'ring her all the reparation in my power.

Har. A fine fcheme truly ! why, Woodville, ar't frantic ?---To predeftinate yourfelf among the horned cattle of Doctors Commons, and take a wife for the very reafon which makes fo many fpend thoufands to get rid of one------

Wood. To withdraw an amiable creature from her duty, without being able to make her happy, is to me a very ferious reflection ;---nay, I finned, I may fay, from *virtue :* and, had I been a lefs grateful fon, might have called myfelf a faultlefs lover.

Har. Well, well, man! you are young enough to truft to time, and he does wonders.---Don't go now and ruin yourfelf with your uncle ;----I have found him out already, and advertife you, none of your formal obfequious bows and refpectful affents will do with him ; having been cheated in former times of half his fortune by a parafite, he miftrufts ev'ry one, and always miftakes politenefs for fervility. Maintain your own opinion, if you would win his; for he generally grows undetermined, the moment he knows thofe around him are otherwife : and, above all, fhake off this mental lethargy.

Wood. I will endeavour to take your advice.---- Should fhe fly I were undone for ever !----but you are no judge of my Cecilia's fincerity. How fhould you know thofe qualities, which rife with ev'ry following hour ?---Can you think fo meanly of me, as that I could be duped by a vulgar wretch? a felfifh wanton?

oh

oh no!---fhe poffeffes every virtue but the one I have
robbed her of.   [*Exit.*

Harcourt *alone.*

Har. Poor Frank! thy fponfors furely, by intui-
tion, characterized thee when they gave thee that name.
----Did I love your welfare lefs, I could foon eafe your
heart, by acquainting you of my marriage with Mifs
Mortimer; but now the immediate confequence would
be this ridiculous match.----How, if I apprize either
my Lord or the Governor? both obftinate in different
ways: I might betray only to ruin him.----A thought
occurs;---my perfon is unknown to her---chufing an
hour when he is abfent, I'll pay her a vifit, offer her an
advantageous fettlement, and learn from her behaviour
her real character and intentions.   .   [*Exit.*

THE END OF THE FIRST ACT.

ACT II.

SCENE, *An elegant Dreſſing-Room, with a Toilette richly ornamented. A Harpſichord, and a Frame with Embroidery.*

Bridget *fetches various ſmall Jars with Flowers, and talks as ſhe places them.*

Brid. LORD help us! how fantaſtical ſome folks not an hundred miles off are! If I can imagine what's come to my lady?---Here has ſhe been ſighing and groaning theſe two months, becauſe her lover was in the country; and now truly, ſhe's ſighing and groaning becauſe he's come to town. Such maggots indeed! I might as well have ſtaid in our pariſh all the days of my life, as to live mew'd up with her in this dear ſweet town: I could but have done that with a *vairtuous* lady---altho' I know ſhe never was at Fox-hall in all her jaunts, and we two ſhould cut ſuch a figure there!---Bleſs me! what's come to the glaſs? (*ſetting her dreſs*) why ſure it's dull'd with her eternal ſighing, and makes me look as frightful as herſelf!--- Oh, here ſhe comes with a face as long, and diſmal, as if he was going to be married, and to ſomebody elſe too.

D

Cecilia

Cecilia enters, and throws herself on the Sopha, leaning on her hand.

Cec. What can detain Woodville fuch an age !---
It is an hour at leaft fince he rode by.   Run, Bridget !
and look if you can fee him through the drawing-room
window.

Brid. Yes, madam.   *(Exit, eyeing her with con-*
tempt.)

Cec. How wearifome is ev'ry hour to the wretched !
---they catch at each future one, merely to while away
the prefent.   For, were Woodville here, could he re-
lieve me from the torment of reflection? or the ftrong,
though filent, acknowledgment my own heart perpe-
tually gives of my error?

Brid. (without) Here he comes, ma'am, here he
comes !

Cec. Does he ?---run down then---*(fluttered.)*

Brid. Dear me, no; 'tis not neither : *(enters)* 'tis
only the French Ambaffador's new cook, with his huge
bag and long ruffles.

Cec. Blind animal !   Sure nothing is fo tormenting
as expectation.

Brid. La, ma'am ! any thing will torment one,
when one has a mind to be tormented ; which muft be
your cafe for certain.   What fignifies fitting mope,
mope, mope, from morning to night ?   You'd find
yourfelf a deal better if you went out only two or three
times a day.---For a walk, we are next door to the
park, as I may fay : and, for a ride, fuch a dear fweet
vis-a-vis and pretty horfes might tempt any one : then,
as to company, you'll fay, " a fig for your ftarch'd
" ladies,

"ladies, who owe their virtue to their uglinefs,"----
mine is very much at your fervice. (*Curtfies*)

Cec. How could I endure this girl, did I not know
that her ignorance exceeds even her impertinence?---
I have no pleafure in going abroad.

Brid. Oh la, ma'am! how fhould you know 'till
you try? Sure ev'ry body muft wifh to fee and be
feen. Then there's fuch a delightful hurricane----all
the world are bufy, tho' moft are doing nothing:----to
fplafh the mob, and drive againft the people of quality;
----oh, give me a coach, and London for ever and ever!
You could but lock yourfelf up, were you as old and
ugly as gay Lady Grizzle at next door.

Cec. Had I been fo, I had continued happy.

Brid. La, ma'am, don't ye talk fo purphanely!
----happy, to be old and ugly?----or, I'll tell you
what, as you don't much feem to fancy going out,
fuppofe you were to come down now and then (you
know we have a pure large hall) and take a game of
romps with *us*? If you were once to fee our Jacob
hunt the flipper, you would die with laughing!----
Madam Frifk (my laft miftrefs) ufed, as foon as ever
mafter was gone, (and indeed he did not trouble her
much with his company) to run down, draw up her
brocaded niggle-de-gee, and fall to play at fome good
fun or other:----dear heart! we were as merry then as
the day was long; I am fure I have never been half fo
happy fince.

Cec. I cannot poffibly imitate the model you pro-
pofe; but tho' *I* don't chufe to go abroad, you may.

Brid.

Brid. I don't love to go much among the mobility neither. If indeed, madam, next winter you'd give me some of your tickets, I would fain go to a masquerade (it vexes me to see um stick in the thing-um-bobs for months together) and Mrs. Trim promises me the lent of a *Wenus's* dress, which, she says, I shall cut a figure in. Now, ma'am, if I had but some diamonds, (for beggars wear diamonds there, they say) who knows but I might make my fortune, like you?

Cec. Mar it, much rather, like me.----That is no place for girls of your station, which exposes you to so much insult.

Brid. Ah, let me alone, madam, for taking care of number one. I ware never afeard but once in my whole life, and that ware of grandfar's ghost; for he always hated I, and used to walk, (poor soul!) in our barken, for all the world like an ass with a tye-wig on.——— *(Knocking hard.)*

Cec. Hark! that sure is Woodville's knock! fly, and see! *(Walks eagerly to the door, and returns as eagerly)*———Alas, is this my repentance? dare I sin against my judgment?

Enter Woodville.

Wood. My Cecilia!---my soul!---have I at last the happiness of beholding you? You know me too well to imagine I would punish *myself* by a moment's voluntary delay.

Cec. Oh, no; it is not that--*(both sit down on the sopha.)*

Wood.

Wood. Say, you are glad to fee me?---afford me one kind word to atone for your cold looks!---are you not well?

Cec. Rather fay I am not happy.----My dear Woodville, I am an altered being: why have you reduced me to fhrink thus in your prefence?---oh, why have you made me unworthy of yourfelf?---(*leans againft his fhoulder weeping.*)

Wood. Cruel girl!---is this my welcome?---when did I appear to think you fo?

Cec. Tell me, when any one elfe will think me otherwife?

Wood. Will you never be above fo narrow a prejudice? are we not the whole world to each other?--- nay, dry your tears! allow me to dry them; (*kiffes her cheek*) what is there, in the reach of love or wealth, I have not fought to make you happy?

Cec. That which is the effence of all enjoyments, ---innocence:----oh, Woodville, you knew not the value of the heart, whofe peace you have deftroyed.---- My fenfibility firft ruined my virtue, and then my repofe.----But, though for you I confented to abandon an humble happy home, to embitter the age of my venerable father, and bear the contempt of the world, I can never fupport my own. My heart revolts againft my fituation, and hourly bids me renounce a fplendor, which only renders guilt more defpicable. (*Rifes*) I meant to explain this hereafter; but the agitation of my mind obliged me to lighten it immediately.

Wood.

Wood. Is your affection then already extinct? for sure it must, when you can resolve to torture me thus.

Cec. Were my love extinct, I might sink into a mean content!---oh no,---'Tis to that alone I owe my resolution.

Wood. Can you then plunge me into despair?---so young, so lovely too!---oh, where could you find so safe an asylum as my heart?---whither could you fly?

Cec. I am obliged to you, sir, for the question; but who is it has made me thus destitute?---I may retain your protection, indeed, but at what a price!

Wood. Give me but a little time, my love! I am equally perplexed between my father and my uncle; each of whom offers me a wife I can never love. Suffer them to defeat each other's schemes!---let me, if possible, be happy without a crime; for I must think it one, to grieve a parent hitherto so indulgent.---I will not put any thing in competition with your peace; and long for the hour when the errors of the lover will be absorb'd in the merits of the husband.

Cec. No, Woodville! that was, when innocent, as far above my hopes, as it is now beyond my wishes.----I love you too sincerely to reap any advantage from so generous an error; yet you at once flatter and wound my heart, in allowing me worthy such a distinction: but love cannot subsist without esteem; and how should I possess your's, when I have lost even my own?

Wood.

Wood. It is impoffible you fhould ever lofe either, while fo deferving both.----I fhall not be fo eafily denied hereafter, but am bound by the caprices of others at prefent.----I am obliged to return directly, but will haften to you the very firft moment;----when we meet again, it muft be with a fmile, remember.

Cec. It will, when we meet again.----Oh how thofe words opprefs me! *(afide)* but do not regulate your conduct by mine, nor make me an argument with yourfelf, for difobeying my Lord; for here I folemnly fwear never to accept you without the joint confent of both our fathers; and that I confider as an eternal ab-juration:----but, may the favor'd woman you are to make happy, have all my love without my weaknefs!

[*Exit in tears.*

Wood. Difinterefted, exalted girl!----why add fuch a needlefs bar? for is it poffible to gain my father's confent? and yet, without her, life would be infup-portable:----the cenfures of the world,—what is that world to me?----were I weak enough to facrifice her to the erroneous judgment of the malicious and unfeel-ing, what does it offer to reward me?---commenda-tions I can never deferve, and riches I can never enjoy.

[*Exit.*

SCENE,

SCENE, *A Street before* Cecilia's *House.*

Jacob opens the Door and lets out Woodville, *who paſſes over the Stage;* Jacob *remains with his Hands in his Pockets, whiſtling.*

Enter Vane, *diſguis'd, with a Baſket of Game in his Hand.*

Vane. So, there he goes at laſt, I may open the attack without fear of a diſcovery, ſince our hopeful heir will hardly return directly----This intelligence of my landlord's of the Blue Poſts has made the matter much eaſier.------Um, a good ſubject!----ſure I ought to know that Bumpkin's face! as I live, my playfellow at the pariſh-ſchool, Jacob Gawky!------now for a touch of the old dialect------d'ye hire, young mon!---prey, do ye knaw where one Bett Dowſon do live?

Jac. Noa; not I.---

Vane. Hay!---why, zure as two-pence, thou beeſt Jacob Gawky!

Jac. Odſbodlikins! zo I be indeed!---but, who beeſt thee?

Vane. What, dooſt not knaw thy ould zkhool-fellow, Wull, mun?

Jac. Hay!---What,---Wull?--- od rabbit it, if I ben't deſprate glad to zee thee, where doo'ſt live now, mun?

Vane. Down at huome, in our pariſh;---I be cóm'd up with Sir Izaac Promiſe, to be meade excoiſe-man?

Jac. Thee'ft good luck, faith! wifh, no odds to thee, my fortin ware as good!---but theed'ft *always* a muortal good notion of wroiting and cyphers, while I don't knaw my own neame when I do zee it.----What didft leave zea for?

Vane. Why, I ware afraid I fhould be killed before I com'd to be a great mon :---but what brought thee into this foine houfe?

Jac. Fortin, Wull! fortin.---Didft thee knaw Nan o' th' Mill?

Vane. Noa, not I.

Jac. Od rabbit it! I thought ev'ry muortal zoul had knawd zhe.---Well, Nan and I ware fuch near neighbors, there ware only a barn between us;----fhe ware a defperate zmart lafs, that's the truth on't : and I had half a moind to teake to feyther's bufinefs, and marry zhe :---but ecod the zimpletony grow'd fo fond, that fome how or other, I ware tired firft! when, behold you, zquire takes a fancy to me, and made I cuome and live at the hall; and, as my head run all on tuown, when aw comed up to London, aw brought I wi' un:---zo I thought to get rid that way of the bullocking of Nan.

Vane. But, Jacob, how didft get into thic fine houfe?

Jac. Dang it, doan't I zeay, I'll tell thee prefent---Zoa, as I ware faying,---one holiday I went to zee thic there church, wi' the top like a huge punch-bowl turned auver; and, dang it! who fhould arrive in the very nick, but madam Nan——well, huome comes I as merry as a cricket;---'fquire caals for I in a muortal hurry; when who fhould I zee, but madam Nan on her marrowbones a croying for dear

E   loife!

loife!—dang it, I thought at firſt I ſhould ha'
zwounded;—zo a made a long zarment about 'ducing
a poor girl, and zaid I ſhould certainly go to the
divil for it, and then turn'd I off. But the beſt fun is
to come, mun;—rabbit me! if aw did not teake Nan
into keeping himſelf; and zhe do flaunt it about, as
foine as a ducheſs!

Vane. A mighty religious moral gentleman, truly!
(Aſide) Well, now you came to this pleace?

Jac. Why, Meay-day, walking in Common Garden to ſmell the pozeys, who zhould I ſee but our
Bridget?—I was muortal glad to zee her, you muſt
needs think, and zhe got I this here place.

Vane. Wounds! doſt live wi' a Lord in this foine
houſe?

Jac. Noa; a Leady, you fool! but ſuch a Leady,
zuch a dear, eaſy, good-natur'd creature!—zhe do
never ſay noa, let we do what we wull.

Vane. Now to the point, *(aſide)* is your Lady
married?

Jac. Noa: but ſhe's as good; and what'ſt think,
mun?—to a Lord's zon!—tho' if a ware a King,
aw would not be too good for zhe.—A mortal fine
comely mon too, who do love her, as aw do the eyes in
his head. Couzin Bridget do tell I, zhe zee'd a letter,
where aw do zay aw wull ha her any day of the week,
whatever do come o'th' next.—Why, I warrant, they
have pointed wedding-day!

Vane. The devil they have? my Lord will go mad
at this news. *(Aſide)*

Jac. Lauk a deazy! how merry we will be on that
day! wot come and junket wi' us?

Vane.

Vane. Yes, yes, I fhall certainly make one among you,—either then or before; (*afide*)—but now I muſt goa and give this geame to zquire—zquire—what the Dickens be his neame? I do *always* forget it,—there zhould be a ticket ſomewhere:—zoa,—rabbit me! if ſome of your London fauk ha' no' cut it off, out o' fun!

Jac. Ha, ha, ha! ecod nothing more likelier,—(*both laugh foolifhly*) thee rum people be zo zharp as needles.—But there's no pleace like it, for all that—I be ſet upon living and dying in it.

Vane. Now to ſecure my return if neceſſary. (*Afide*) —I'll tell thee what, Jacob! feeing as how I ha loſt thic there direction, do thee teake the baſket: 'tis only a preſent of geame from the parſon o' our pariſh; and, if zo be I can't find the gentleman, why 'tis ho-neſtly mine.—Meay be I'll come, and teake a bit o' ſupper wi' ye.

Jac. Wull ye indeed?—dang it! that's clever; and then you'll fee our Bridget. She's a mortal zmart laſs, I promiſe ye!—and, meay be, may'ſt get a peep at my Lady, who's deſperate handſome!—good bye t'ye. —Bridget's zo comical!—od rabbit it, we'll be main merry, [*Exit.*

Vane *alone.*

Vane. Thus far I have ſucceeded to admiration!—our young heir has really a mind to play the fool and marry his miſtreſs!—tho', faith, marrying *his own* does not ſeem very inexcuſable, when ſo many of his

E 2 equals

equals modeftly content themfelves with the caft-offs' of
half *their acquaintance.*   [*Exit.*

SCENE, *An Apartment in* Cecilia's *Houfe.*

Enter Bridget.

Brid. So, juft the old ftory again ! crying, crying
for ever !—Lord, if I was a man, I fhould hate fuch a
whimpering—what would fhe have, I wonder ? to
refufe fuch a handfome, genteel, good-natur'd man !—
and, I'll be fworn, he offer'd to marry her ; for I
liftened with all my ears !—oh, that he would have *me*
now !—I fhould become my own coach purdigioufly,
that's a fure thing. Hay, who knocks ?

Enter Jacob.

Jac. A young man do want my Leady.

Brid. A man ?—what fort of a man ?

Jac. Why a man—like—juft fuch another as I.

Brid. No, no, no ;—that's not fo eafy to find :—
what can any man want with her ? fhew him in here,
Jacob.

Jac. (Returning in a kind of glee) When fhall we
have the wedding, Bridget ?

Brid. We fhall have a burying firft, I believe.

Jac. Od rabbit it ! we won't be their feconds there,
faith !   [*Exit.*

Brid. Now, if he miftakes me for my Lady, I fhall
find out what he wants.

                                          Enter

Enter Captain Harcourt, *disguised, with* Jacob.

Har. (*Surveying her*)——Is *that* your Lady?

Jac. He, he, he! lauk, zur, don't ye knaw that's our *Bridget?* - [*Exit.*

Brid. So, deuce on him, there's my whole scheme spoilt!—my Lady, sir, is engaged; but, if you tell me your business, it will do just as well.

Har. For yourself it may, child! (*chucks her under the chin.*)

Brid. What, you belong to Mr. Gargle the apothecary? or come from the jeweller on Ludgate-hill? or have a letter from——

Har. (*Interrupting her.*)—The very person; you have hit it. And now, do me the favour to tell your Lady, a *stranger* wishes to speak to her on particular business.

Brid. Very well, sir:——was ever handsome man so crabbed! [*Exit.*

Har. Egad, if the mistress have half as much tongue as the maid, Woodville may catch me in the midst of my first speech.——Now for my credentials! and here she comes!——a lovely girl indeed! I can scarce blame Frank, for she awes *me.*

Enter Cecilia, *followed officiously by* Bridget,

Cec. I was informed, sir, you had particular business with me?

Har. I took the liberty, madam,——I say, madam, I——

Cec.

Cec. As I have neither friends or relations in London, *(sighs)* I am at a loss to guess————

Har. What I would communicate, madam, requires secrecy.

Cec. Bridget, go where I ordered you just now.

Brid. Yes, madam;———but if I an't even with you for this.   [*Exit.*

Cec. I complied with your request, Sir, without enquiring the motive; because you, I think, *can* have only one———My father, if I may trust my heart, has made you his messenger to an unwilling offender.

Har. Pardon me, madam, but I refer you to this.

Cec. (*Reads*)

" Madam,

" Being certainly informed Mr. Woodville is on the point of marrying a Lady chosen by his friends, when it is presumed you will be disengaged, a nobleman of rank, and estate above what *he* can ever possess, is thus early in laying his heart and fortune at your feet, lest some more lucky rival should anticipate him.————
The bearer is authorised to disclose all particulars, and offer you a settlement worthy your acceptance.————
Deign, madam, to listen to him on the subject, and you will find the unknown lover as generous and not less constant than Woodville."

Cec. Good heavens! to what an insult have I exposed myself! [*She bursts into tears, and sinks into a chair, without minding* Harcourt; *who watches her with irresolution.*]

Har. What can I think?———there is an air of injur'd delicacy in her, which teaches me to reproach myself for a well-meant deceit.————If, madam,————

                                                          Cec.

Cec. I had forgot this wretch. *(Rises)* Return, fir, to your vile employer; tell him, whoever he is, I am too fenfible of the infult, tho' not entitled to refent it—tell him, I have a heart above my fituation, and that he has only had the barbarous fatisfaction of adding another mifery to thofe which almoft overwhelmed me before.

Har. Hear me, madam, I conjure you!

Cec. Never! a word would contaminate me.—— *(Struggling to go off.)*

Har. Nay, you fhall——You do not know half the good confequences of this letter; I am the friend, the relation of Woodville—my name Harcourt!

Cec. Is it poffible *he* fhould be fo cruel, fo un-juft——

Har. He is neither cruel nor unjuft, but only un-fortunate.----Hear---he defigns to marry you; this I learnt from himfelf only this morning. As a proof of my fincerity, I will own I doubted your right to that mark of his efteem, and made this trial in confequence. Pleas'd to find you worthy of his rank, I feel fhock'd at reminding you, you ought not to fhare it. But, madam, if you truly love him, you cannot wifh that to be juft to you, he fhould be unjuft to thofe who have a prior right over him.----This fhall pofitively be my laft effort. *(Afide)*

Cec. A motive like your's, fir, will excufe any thing. How little my happinefs, honour, or intereft, *ever* weighed againft his, need not be repeated. Far be it from me *now* to difgrace him; he is apprized of my invincible objections to a match which will never

take

take place. May he form a happier, while I by a voluntary poverty expiate my offence.

Har. Ma----- Ma---- what the devil choaks me
so?---I am struck with your sentiments, and must find
you a proper asylum. The moment I saw you, I had
hopes such manners could not veil an immoral heart.
I have proved your sincerity, and owe a reparation to
your delicacy. The proposed bride of Woodville is
every way worthy that distinction; nor am I without
hopes even *she* will be prevailed on to protect you.----
But I must not leave a doubt of my sincerity:---do you
know Miss Mortimer?

Cec. I have seen the lady, sir. But dare I credit
my senses?----has heav'n form'd two such hearts, and
for me?----

Har. With her, your story will be buried for ever:
and, I think, the sooner you disappear, the more ea-
sily will you prevent Woodville's disobedience. I will
open the affair to Miss Mortimer directly, and, if she
acquiesces, desire her to call for you in person, to prevent the possibility of any artifice.

Cec. He, who inspired such sentiments, alone can
reward them! Oh, sir, you have raised a poor de-
sponding heart; but it shall be the business of my future life to deserve those favours I can never half re-
pay.

Har. I find, by punishing me with acknowledg-
ments, you are resolved to be obliged to me. The
time is too precious to be wasted on such trifles. At
seven, you shall have certain intelligence of my suc-
cefs:

cefs : employ the interim to the beft advantage, and hope every thing from daring to deferve well.

[*Exit.*

Cecilia *alone.*

Aftonifhing interpofition of heav'n!---Hope?--- what have I to hope?--- but, let the confcioufnefs of acting rightly fupport me in the fad moment of re- nouncing Woodville; and, in him, all that render'd life defirable.

SCENE, *Lord* Glenmore's Houfe.

Lord Glenmore *and* Vane.

L. Glen. And are you fure of all this?

Vane. Abfolutely, my Lord! I have known the bumpkin, her footman, from the height of his own club.

L. Glen. What a curs'd infatuation!---thefe are the comforts of children;---our fears beginning, from the moment our power ends;---the happieft of fathers is not to be envied;---I know not what to re- folve on!

Vane. If I may be permitted to advife, my Lord---

L. Glen. And who afk'd your advice, fir?

Vane. You have, my Lord,-- formerly.

L. Glen. Take care you ftay 'till I do! leave me, fir.

F

Vane.

Vane. If you don't like my advice, I shall give you my opinion very shortly.----A crusty crab !

[*Exit muttering.*

L. Glen. This is the certain confequence of entrust-ing low people ;---and yet there is no doing without them.----I can never master my feelings enough to speak properly to Woodville on the subject, therefore must fix on some other method---*(paufes)*---That's a sure one, and falls heavy on the artful, afpiring creature, only !---Vane !---

Re-enter Vane.

----Could not you procure me a travelling-chaife and four stout fellows immediately ?

Vane. To be fure, my Lord, I can order a chaife at any inn, if you chufe it.

L. Glen. Pho, pho,---don't put on that face ;---you must go through with this thing like a man.----Here's fomething for the share you have already had in it.----Do what I have ordered, and wait near the Horfe Guards in about an hour ; when I shall feize this infolent baggage, and convey her out of my son's reach;---You gave me a high-flown account of her ; ---and, as you are a fmart young fellow, and she must at leaft be pretty, if we can contrive to frighten her into taking *you* as a hufband, it will end all my fears, and shall be the making of your fortune.

Vane. Gad, I like the project well.----A handfome wife is the beft bait, when we fish for preferment ;---and this gives me a double claim both on father and son. *(afide)* Nothing but the profound refpect I have

for

for your Lordſhip could induce me to think of this;
—though born without rank and fortune, I have a ſoul,
my Lord,——

L. Glen. Come, come; my good lad! I gueſs
what you would ſay: but we have no time for
ſpeeches.——I have ſet my heart on the ſucceſs of this
project; and you ſhall find your intereſt in indulging
me.   [*Exeunt different ways.*

SCENE, *Miſs* Mortimer's *Apartment.*

Enter Captain Harcourt, *meeting Miſs* Mortimer.

Har. If I were to judge of your temper by your
looks, my dear, I ſhould ſay it was uncommonly ſweet
this morning.

M. Mor. A truce with compliment; I muſt, in
reaſon, renounce dear flattery after marriage.

Har. To flattery you never paid court: but the
language of the heart and the world will ſometimes
reſemble.—I ought, however, to praiſe your temper,
for I am come to try it,——and give you a noble opportunity of exerting its benevolence.

M. Mor. A benevolence you certainly doubt, by
this ſtudied eulogium.

Har. I might, did I not know it well.——In ſhort,
my love, I have taken the ſtrangeſt ſtep this morning——

M. Mor. What ſtep, for heav'n's ſake?

Har. In regard to a lady.——

M. Mor. Not another wife, I hope?

Har. No,——only a miſtreſs.——

M. Mor. Oh, a trifle; a trifle.——

Har.

Har. You may laugh, madam, but I am ſerious ; and a fine girl ſhe is : nay to ſhew you I have not read Cheſterfield in vain, I have robb'd my deareſt friend of her; in plain Engliſh, Woodville has a miſtreſs he doats on ſo madly, as even to intend marrying her.----Imagining her, like moſt of her ſtamp, only an artful and intereſted creature, I paid her a viſit as a ſtranger, with an offer which muſt have unveil'd her heart, had it been baſe :---but I found her, on the contrary, a truly noble-minded girl, and far above her preſent ſituation ; which ſhe earneſtly wiſhes to quit.--- In ſhort, my dear, I thought it prudent to part them; and, in your name, offered her an aſylum.

M. Mor. In my name? You amaze me, Mr. Harcourt ! Would you aſſociate your wife with a kept miſtreſs ? bring ſuch an acquiſition into the houſe of Lord Glenmore, and deprive Woodville of perhaps his only reaſon for not interfering with us ?---Do you think I credit this *ſudden* acquaintance ?

Har. I deceiv'd myſelf, I find :—I thought you above ſuch low ſuſpicion, that you could make diſtinctions.

M. Mor. Yes, yes, I can make diſtinctions more clearly than you wiſhed. You muſt excuſe my interference in this affair, ſir ; and let me hint to you, that your own will do as little credit to your heart as to your underſtanding.

Har. Mighty well, madam ; go on ! Settle this with reſpect to yourſelf, but do not be concerned about me ; for, in one word, if you cannot reſolve on protecting this poor unfortunate, I will.

4   *M. Mor.*

M. Mor. (*Aside*) That muſt not be ; yet his warmth alarms me.----Nay but, my dear, think deliberately !---Suppoſing her all you ſay, the world judges by actions, not thoughts, and will bury her merit in her ſituation.

Har. It is that cruel argument perpetuates error in ſo many of your frail ſex : be the firſt to riſe above it. That you are in Lord Glenmore's houſe, will be your juſtification, both to the world and himſelf : for, what but a generous motive can actuate you ? In my eyes, my dear Sophia, virtue never looks ſo lovely as when ſhe ſtretches out her hand to the fallen.

M. Mor. Oh, Harcourt ! I am aſhamed of my ſuſpicion : I ought to have known all the candour and generoſity of your heart, and received in a moment the unhappy woman it patronized :---yet, at this criſis, in our own affairs to run the chance of further exaſperating my benefactor————

Har. I am not to learn, that friendſhip and love have been mere maſks to fraud and folly in the great world ; no one would blame me, were I to ſuffer Woodville to ruin himſelf, as the ſhorteſt way of fixing my own fortune, and obtaining my Lord's approbation of your choice. But, I know not how it happened, that, when a mere boy, I took it into my head, truth was as much to the purpoſe as lying ; and, as I never got into more ſcrapes than others, why I ſtill purſue my ſyſtem, and prefer honour to art. Then, if we fail, we have ſomething better to conſole us than a pond or a piſtol ; and, if we ſucceed, what is there wanting to our happineſs ?

M. Mor-

M. Mor.   And how do you mean to manage her escape?

Har.   That, my deareft, is the difficulty. I found fhe had feen you, and therefore was obliged to fatisfy her of my honour, by affuring her you would call for her in perfon.

M. Mor.   Very well; we muft carefully watch our opportunity. You dine here---the *word* of command you are accuftomed to obey, but you muft now become obedient to the *look:* for, you know, I have my difficulties, however ftrong my defire of obliging you.

[*Exeunt.*

END OF THE SECOND ACT.

A C T   III.

SCENE I. *A magnificent Drawing-Room.*

Miss Mortimer *pouring out Coffee sends it to the Company;* Captain Harcourt *leans against a Pannel near her, sipping it; at a little Distance the* Governor *and* Woodville *playing at Backgammon, while Lord* Glenmore *leans over his Chair, thoughtfully observing the Behaviour of his Son, who loses merely to make his Uncle leave off.*

Har. IT grows near the appointed hour, my love !---but how to make sure of Woodville.

M. Mor. You should have thought of that before, my sagacious confidante ! However, as I do not need your company, fasten it upon him ;---pretend a duel,---pretend an intrigue ;---in short, if all else fails, pretend you are dying, and keep him to make your will, rather than suffer him to interrupt me.

L. Glen. (*to himself*) What way can I secure the absence of this son of mine ? for, I see plainly, another lucky hit would almost provoke him into throwing the dice in the Governor's face : yet Vane, I doubt, has hardly been able to procure me ev'ry convenience in so short a time. However, I will make one of my own garrets his minx's prison, rather than suffer her to interfere with my serious views.

Gov.

Gov. (*Rifing from play*) Zounds, Frank! you are like the French; fo ready to be beat, that there is hardly any triumph in conquering you. But you fhall take your revenge, I infift upon it.

Wood. Another time, fir;---my head achs;---my ----in fhort, I cannot play any longer; my coufin will engage with you.

Har. (*twitching his fleeve*) Kind fir, your coufin is infinitely indebted to you; but he, like yourfelf, may have fomething elfe to do; and fo indeed has ev'ry body, for we all feem impatient to feparate.

M. Mor. (*to the fervant, removing coffee*) Bid Warner fend my cloak.

L. Glen. Going abroad, my dear ?

M. Mor. Only a formal round, my Lord.

L. Glen. Woodville, you attend Mifs Mortimer.

M. Mor. Sweetly contrived that, however, and my lover feems pofed. (*Afide to* Harcourt)---I will not fo feverely tax Mr. Woodville's politenefs, my Lord.

Wood. You are very obliging, madam; (*to Harcourt*) and the only thing fhe has faid or done to oblige me this day, entre nous.

Har. (*afide*) Um, not quite fure of that, if you knew all---(*turning to Mifs* Mortimer) I will march off quietly, and lie in wait for Woodville, fo that I think you may depend on his not meeting you.

[*Goes off unobferved.*

[Woodville, *having taken his hat and fword, offers his hand to Mifs* Mortimer.

L. Glen. So, he is going to efcape! They all take pleafure in perplexing me. Frank, return to me di- rectly;

rectly; I have bethought myself of fomething very important, in which I need your affiftance.

Wood. Would I had bethought myfelf of vanifhing, like Harcourt! How devilifhly vexatious!

[*Leads Mifs Mortimer off.*

Gov. So, there goes madam, to coquette, curtfy, and talk nonfenfe with every well-dreffed ape of either fex. Before I would allow a girl fuch a freedom---

L. Glen. Brother, do not judge 'till you know her and give me leave to tell you, thefe prejudices of your temper will render you very ridiculous.

Gov. The prejudices of *my* temper! Oh Lord, Oh Lord! this is an excellent jeft. Zounds, becaufe you have not the ufe of your eyes.---

L. Glen. I fhall never have patience. My head is juft now full of fomething too important, to examine which of us is moft in the wrong. I am fixed on removing this ambitious minx of my fon's for ever out of his reach immediately. Will you oblige me with the company of your fervants? Being flaves, they will not dare reveal the affair; and, were they fo inclined, can hardly comprehend it.

Gov. Will I? ay, that I will; and with my own company into the bargain.

L. Glen. Hift! he returns; and, if we may judge by his countenance, mortified enough, to lofe the evening away from her.

Re-enter Woodville.

Go, my dear Frank, firft to Puzzle's chambers, for

G   the

the mortgage of Hayfield house, and don't fail to learn his whole opinion upon the subject; *(aside to the* Governor*)* and that will take two long hours by a very moderate computation;---then proceed to the London Tavern, and ask if Levi, the Jew, waits there by my appointment? otherwise do you wait there 'till either he or I join you.

Wood. A pretty round-about employment my father has invented for me! *(aside)* and I dare not give the least symptoms of disgust, lest that troublesome old uncle of mine should pry into the cause. I shall observe your orders, my Lord---though if the devil has called upon the counsellor a little before his time, I shall consider it as an eternal obligation.   [*Exit.*

L. Glen. Now I must enquire after Vane.   [*Exit.*

Gov. And I will give a little lecture to my myrmidons, and wait with them your pleasure. Od, it will be precious sport, to catch madam so unawares, and see her play off every virtuous grimace with which she entangled young 'Scapegrace.   [*Exeunt severally.*

S C E N E, *The Hall.*

Enter Vane, *looking about.*

Hey-day; sure his old-fashioned Lordship has not employed two of us on one errand! An old man has been hov'ring about madam's house, and has followed me here, without my knowing what to make of him. However, ears befriend me!   [*Retires listening.*
                                                    Enter

Enter the Governor, *and his black Servants soon after.*

Here Anthony, Pompey, Cæsar! you dogs, be ready to attend my Lord and me on a little expedition. ---No; no flambeaus, boobies!---the chaste Miss Diana will surely take a spiteful pleasure in lighting us to catch another kind of Miss.---And, do ye hear? not one syllable of the when, where, or how, except you intend to dangle on one string, like a bunch of black grapes.   [*Talks to them apart.*

Enter Grey.

Grey. It is here, I am at length informed, the father of this abandoned seducer resides.---Yet, what redress can poverty hope from pride?---surely, however, for his own sake, he will assist me in regaining the poor girl, and afterwards prevent the wretch from pursuing her?---there I suppose he is!--- my Lord.

Gov. (*Turns short upon him*) Well, old sturdy! what do you want with my Lord?

Grey.---Merciful heav'n! the father of Cecilia

Vane. (*Listening*) Hey?--- indeed!

Grey. Oh! how my heart misgives me! perhaps, this base Woodville--- her very brother----

Gov. What, is the old man ill?---sure I know this honest---it is not---yet it is---Grey?

Grey. The same indeed, my Lord.

Gov. No my Lord, to me, man! my name is Harcourt.

Grey.

Grey. Blessed be heav'n for that however !

Gov. Be not righteous over much ! for that my name is Harcourt, I do not reckon among the first favours of heav'n.----But, ha, ha ! perhaps you thought I had no name at all by this time ?---'faith, I put a pretty trick upon---well, well, well !---(*to the blacks*) you may retire till my Lord is ready.   [*Exeunt.*
I am a riddle, honest Grey ! but now I am come to expound myself, and make thy fortune into the bargain.----It is many a long day since I saw old England. ----But at last I am come home with a light heart and a heavy purse, design to fetch up my Cicely, give her and my money to the honestest fellow I can find, and grow old amid' a rosy race of Britons springing from a stem rear'd after my own fashion.---There's news for you, my honest friend.

Grey. Alas, how little will he think I deserve his favour, when he hears my account of her ! and how can I shock a parent, with what too severely shocks even myself ?   [*Aside.*

Gov. What,--silent, man ?--ha, ha, ha ! I can't but laugh to think how foolish you look'd at the second year's end, when no allowance came,---but that was my own contrivance: all done on purpose, my good old soul ! and now it will come in a lump; there's the whole difference.---Well, and so my dame made her a pattern of housewifery, hey ?--od ! I don't intend to touch another pickle or preserve that is, not of my little Cicely's own doing ; and I'll build her a dairy with ev'ry bowl and churn of silver !---zounds, it shall be a finer sight than the Tower of London !---

and

ar we'll set up dame Deborah's statue before it, like Queen Ann's in St. Paul's Church-yard!---but, why doft'nt enjoy this discov'ry, man? ar't afraid I shall take her from thee? oh, never think of that; for thou shalt bless ev'ry pye she makes; ay, and *taste* it afterwards, Old Pudding-Sleeves.

Grey. Ah, sir! *(sighing.)*

Gov. Hey? Zounds!---what do'st mean? sure my Cicely isn't dead?

Grey. No, not dead, sir!

Gov. She's very near it, then, I suppose?

Grey. No, Sir.

Gov. No, Sir? then what the devil do you mean by alarming me thus, with your " No Sirs," after all?

Grey. Alas, is there no greater evil?

Gov. None, that I know of; but your whole fraternity are not more like ravens in colour than note; ---come, let us know what this mighty evil is?

Grey. For years did she increase in goodness as in beauty; the charm of ev'ry young heart, and the sole comfort of those old ones, to whom heav'n and man seem'd to have consign'd her for ever.

Gov, Well, well; I had a little bird told me all this----

Grey. About a twelvemonth ago, during a little absence of mine, a young man of fashion introduced himself into my house: and, my wife being void of suspicion, and the dear girl uninstructed in the ways of this bad world,---

Gov.

Gov. The dog betray'd her?---and is this your care, you old------and that ignoramus, your wife---zounds! I am in such a fury;---I want to know no more of her infamous conduct.---Od! I am strangely tempted to have you strangled this moment, as a just reward for your negligence; and so bury the secret with you.

Grey. It is as effectually buried already, Sir,---I love the dear unhappy girl too well, ever to tell her heav'n gave her to such a father.

Gov. Yes, yes;---you are better suited to the---I hope she pays for this severely! you make her stand in a white sheet, to be pointed at by the whole village ev'ry Sunday, to be sure?

Grey. Alas, Sir, she put it out of my power even to forgive her.---

Gov. Forgive her! forgive her truly!

Grey. By flying immediately from her only friend. ---Infirm and poor, I struggled with the joint-evils till now; when, having collected enough to support me, I walk'd up in search of her:---it was only yesterday I discovered her in a splendid coach, which I traced to her house.

Gov. A *house*, I shall run mad entirely---a *coach?* ---why dare the little brazen-face pretend to elegance, when I took such pains to quench ev'ry spark of gentility in her?

Grey. In the neighbourhood I discover'd the name of her seducer; and, in seeking him, met with you.------ Moderate your passion, Sir,------reflect! when age is frail, what can we expect in youth?---shall man desert humanity?

Gov.

Gov. So, fo, fo; now I am to be tortur'd with your preaching.---I renounce the unworthy little flut. ---I have no friend,---no daughter,---no any thing; ---od! I would fooner build an hofpital for ideots, like Swift, and endow it with all my fortune, than beftow it on one who thus perverts reafon:---hark ye, Sir,--- forget the way to this Houfe!---forget you ever faw my face!---would I had never feen your's!---for, if you dare to fend her whining to me, I'll torment you with ev'ry plague, power, wealth, law, or even lawyers can fet in motion---by heav'n, I abjure the audacious little wretch for ever! and will fooner return to India and bury my gold with thofe from whom it was taken, than beftow a fingle fhilling on her, when fhe lofes her *coach* and her *houfe.*

Grey. *(Contemptuoufly)* And I will fooner want a fhilling, than fuffer her to wafte her youth in a ftate which will render her age an unfupportable burthen. Fear not, Sir, ever feeing *her* or *me* again; for the bofom which rear'd will joyfully receive her, nor further embitter her remaining days with the knowledge fhe was born the equal of her undoer; and depriv'd herfelf of all thofe bleffings heav'n only bid, never denied her.   *[Exit.*

Governor *alone.*

Gov. Who would have a daughter?---zounds! I am as hot as if I was in the black hole at *Calcutta.*--- If mifs had only married a lout, from ignorance of her birth, I could have forgiven it; but, her puppy be-

3   ing

ing of fashion, the papers will get hold of it, and I
shall be paragraphed into purgatory.---Fools can turn
wits on these occasions; and " a certain Governor and
his daughter," will set the grinners in motion from
Piccadilly to Aldgate.---This insolent old fellow too!
---I need not wonder were she got courage!---not
but I like his spirit,---od! I like it much!---it proves
his innocence.---What the devil did I drive him away
for!---here, dogs! run after that old man in black, and
order him to return to me this moment.

Enter Lord Glenmore.

L. Glen.   And now brother I am ready for you.

Gov.   Yes; and now, brother, I have something else
to mind, and my servants, moreover.---   [*Exit.*

L. Glen.   What new whim can this troublesome mortal have taken into his head? *(a rapping at the door)*.
I'm not at home remember---Miss Mortimer!--who's
with her?

Miss Mortimer *enters, with* Cecilia *in mourning.*

Miss Mor.   Nay, as to that circumstance---bless
me, here's my Lord!

Cec.   My Lord!--good heav'ns, I shall sink into the
earth!

M. Mor.   He can never guess at you;---recover,
my dear creature!

L. Glen.   Is the lady indispos'd, Miss Mortimer?

M. Mor.   Yes, my Lord;---that is, no---I don't
know what I am saying;---she has been ill lately, and
riding has a little overcome her; that's all.---(*Aside to*
                                          Cecilia)

Cecilia) Struggle to keep up, for heaven's fake and your own.

Cec. Impoffible! (*Lord* Glenmore *draws a hall-chair, in which fhe faints*).

L. Glen. Warner! drops and water, in a moment! ---How beautiful fhe is!---her features are exquifitely fine!

M. Mor. They are thought fo, my Lord.---Blefs me! where can I have crammed my Eau de Luce!--- oh, I have it.

L. Glen. Her pulfe returns,---fhe revives.

Cec. I beg your pardon, madam!---my Lord, too! ---I am fhock'd to have occafioned fo much trouble.

M. Mor. Abfurd, to apologize for the infirmity of nature:---my Lord, I do affure you, was quite anxious---

L. Glen. The man muft furely have loft every fenfe, who can fee this lady, even when deprived of her's, without emotion:---but to me, the languor of illnefs had ever fomething peculiarly interefting.--- (*Afide*) I wonder who this elegant creature is! her hand feems to tremble ftrangely.

Cec. Oh, madam!---

M. Mor. Silence and recollection alone, can fecure you from fufpicion;---I confefs, I relied on his abfence.

Re-enter the Governor.

Gov. He *won't* return, hey?---od! I like the old Cambrian the better for it:---I have fired his Welch blood finely.---Why, what a blockhead was I, not to

H   go

go after him myfelf!---methinks, I fhould like to know mifs, when I meet her in her *coach* too,--um---did he not tell me fomething of tracing the feducer into this houfe! (*ftands in amazement a moment, then whiftles*) *Woodville's* miftrefs, by every thing contrary! od, I fhall feize the gypfy with redoubled fatisfaction! but I muft keep my own counfel, or my old beau of a brother will roaft me to death on my fyftem of education.---Hey! who has he got there? (Cecilia *rifes*) a pretty lafs, faith!--- ah, *there* is the very thing I admire!---there is gentility, without tho fantaftical flourifhes of fafhion!---juft the very air I hoped my minx would have had. (*Lord* Glenmore, *having led off* Cecilia, *returns*).

L. Glen. I don't know how, but my inclination to this bufinefs is over. I think I'll let the matter alone at prefent.

Gov. The devil you will;---why, by to-morrow, Woodville may have married her.

L. Glen. D' ye think fo?---well, then let's go.

Gov. And, what d'ye mean to do with her, pray?

L. Glen. (*afide*) I won't truft this weathercock 'till all is fafe.---I care not what becomes of her, fo fhe is out of my way;---fend her to bridewell, perhaps!

Gov. To Bridewell, truly?---no, that you fhan't neither; Bridewell, quotha!---why, who knows but the fault may be all that young Rakehell your fon's?

L. Glen. My fon's, fir! let me tell you, I have not bred him in fuch a manner,

Gov.

Gov. Oh, if *breeding* were any fecurity-----zounds,
I fhall betray all by another word!　　　(*afide*)

L. Glen. What *now* can have changed you?---but
you are more inconftant than our climate.---Did you
ever know one minute what you fhou'd think the next?
however, to fatisfy your fcruples, I intend to difpatch
her to a nunnery: and, if that don't pleafe you,
e'en take charge of her yourfelf.　　[*Exeunt together.*

Vane *comes forward.*

Vane. Ha, ha, ha; why, this would make a comedy!---and fo, of all birds in the air, his dignified
Lordfhip has pitched on me for the hufband of the
Governor's daughter and his own niece!---well, if I
can but go thro' with this, it will be admirable!---
thank'd by one for making my fortune, and fafe from
the anger of all.

Enter a Servant.

Ser. Mr. Woodville, Sir, is juft gone into the houfe
you bad me watch.　　　　　　　　　[*Exit.*

Vane. The devil he is!---why then I muft confign
my intended to him for one more night, and perfuade
my Lord to delay our feizure 'till morning;---for, to
meet with him would certainly produce an agreement
of all parties, and a marriage which would never en-
roll my name in the family-pedigree, or governor's
will.　　　　　　　　　　　　　　　[*Exit.*

H 2　　　　　SCENE,

SCENE, Cecilia's *Dressing-room.*

Candles burning, and her Clothes scatter'd.

Enter Woodville.

Thanks to that dear lawyer's lucky absence, I have a few happy hours, my love, to spend with thee——— [*looks at her clothes*] already retired? sure I have not left my key in the garden gate.---No, here it is [*rings the bell and takes off his sword, then throws himself into a chair.*] Nobody answer----I don't understand this. ---Perhaps I shall disturb her,---I'll steal into her chamber---[*goes off and presently returns disordered*] not there!---her clothes too, the same she had on last! ---oh, my heart misgives me!---but where are all the servants? [*rings very violently, calling at the same time,* Bridget! Robert! Jacob!]

Enter Bridget, *with her hat on.*

——Bridget! what's become of your Lady?

Brid. Really, Sir, I can't say;——don't you know?

Wood. If I did I shou'd n't have ask'd you.

Brid. (*After a little pause*) Why, sure, Sir, my Lady has not run away? and yet something runs in my head, as if she had.---I thought that spark came for no good to-day.

Wood. What spark, girl?

Brid. Why, just after you went away, comes a young man, a monstrous genteel one and very handfome

some too, I muſt needs ſay; with fine dark eyes and a
freſh colour.

Wood. Damn his colour! tell me his buſineſs.

Brid. So he axed for my Lady, and would not
tell *me* what he wanted: I came with her, however,
but ſhe no ſooner ſet eyes on him than ſhe ſent me out;
which argufi'd no good, you'll ſay; and, before I
could poſſibly come back, though I ran as faſt as ever
my legs could carry me, he was gone, and ſhe writing
and crying for dear life;---but that was no news, ſo
I did not mind it: and when ſhe gave me leave to
go to the play, thought no more harm than the child
unborn.

Wood. It muſt be a ſcheme beyond all doubt, and I
am the dupe of a diſſembling, ungrateful-----oh Cecilia! *(throws himſelf in a chair).*

Brid. *(Softening her voice and ſetting her dreſs)* If I
was as you, Sir, I would not fret about her :---there is
not a lady in the land would ſlight a gentleman ſo handſome and ſweet temper'd---I ſcorns to flatter, for my
part.---Inferials muſt'nt direct their betters : but, had
I been in my Lady's place, a King upon his throne
would not have tempted me.---Handſome him that
handſome does, ſay I; and I am ſure you did handſome
by her; for, if ſhe could have eat gold, ſhe might have
had it.---He might take ſome notice truly.

[*Aſide.*

Wood. *(Starting up)* Where was ſhe writing?
Brid. In the little drawing-room, Sir.

Exit Woodville.

Bridget

Bridget *alone.*

This ridiculous love turns peoples brains, I think.
---I am sure I said enough to open his eyes:---but,
may be, I don't look so handsome, because I am not
so fine.---Hey,---a thought strikes me! my Lady is
gone, that's plain.---Back she will not come, is as
plain. (*Gathers together* Cecilia's *elegant clothes.*) I'll
put on these, and he'll think she gave 'em to me:---
then he may find out, I am as pretty as she: if not---
he and I are of very different opinions.   [*Exit.*

Re-enter Woodville, *more diforder'd.*

Wood.   Cruel, ungrateful, barbarous girl!---to for-
fake me in the very moment I was resolving to facrifice ev'ry thing to her!---but 'tis juft.---Firft dupes
to the arts of man, the pupil soon knows how to foil
him at his own weapons. Perhaps the difcov'ry is
fortunate. In a fhort time, I muft have borne the whole
difgrace of her ill conduct, and my father's refentment
had the bittereft aggravation.---But is fhe indeed gone?
and will continual to-morrows come, without one hope
to render them welcome?

Enter Jacob.

Wood.   Villain! where's your Lady?
Jac.   'Las a deazy, how can I tell, zur?
Wood.   Where are all your fellows?
Jac.   Abroad, making halliday.

Wood.

Wood. When did you go out? who gave you ave?

Jac. My Leady, her own zelf; and I'll tell you how 'tware.---After dinner I geed her a noate; and, when zhe had red un, zhe axed me if zo be as how I had ever zeed the lions? zoa I told her noa; nor no mour I never did.---Zoa zhe geed me half a crown, and bid me goa and make myfelf happy. I thought it ware defperate koind of her; zoa I went and zeed the huge creturs; and ater, only ftop'd a bit to peap at the moniment, and hay my fortin tould by Conj'rer in the Old Bailey; and aw zaid---,

Wood. What the devil does it fignify to me what he faid?---Hark'e, fir, I fee in your face you know more of your miftrefs?

Jac. Dang it, then my feace do lye hugely!

Wood. Tell me the whole truth villain! or I'll ftab you to the heart this inftant.   (*Draws his fword*)

Jac. (*kneels*) I wull, zur, indead I wull: doan't ye terrify me zo! I do forget ev'ry thing in the whole world.

Wood. Be fincere, and depend upon my rewarding you.

Jac. Why, I wifh I meay die this maument, if conj'rer did not zey I fhould lofe my pleace! nay, aw do verily think aw zaid zomething o'my being put in fear o' my loife. Loard knaws, I little thought how zoon his words would come to pafs.

Wood. Will you dally?

Jac. Zoa, as I zaid, zur, when I com'd huome again, I found all the duors aupen, and not a zoul to be zeed,

Wood

Wood. (*aside* This fellow can never mean to impofe on me, and I muft think it a plann'd affair.----While I was in the country, Jacob, did your miftrefs fee much company?

Jac. Cuompany ;--noa, not to fpeak of,---not gentlewomen.

Wood. Gentlewomen! blockhead! why had fhe any male vifitors?

Jac. Anan!

Wood. I muft brain thee at laft, booby! Did any *men* come to fee her then?

Jac. Oh yes, zur, yes---two gentlemen com'd almoft ev'ry deay.

Wood. How, *two* gentlemen? I fhall run diftracted! Young, and handfome?

Jac. Not auver young, zur, nor auver handfome; but dreft mortal foine.

Wood. So they came almoft ev'ry day?--very pretty indeed, Mifs Cecilia!---was you never call'd up while they ftaid?---did they come together or alone?

Jac. Aloane.

Wood. I thought as much; yes, I thought as much. But was you never call'd up, Jacob?

Jac. Yes, zur, when one aw um ware here one deay, I ware caal'd up for zomething or other.

Wood. Well? why don't you go on? I am on the rack!

Jac. Don't ye look fo mortal angry then?

Wood. Well, well, I won't, my good fellow!----there's money for thy honefty.

Jac. Well ;---there aw ware---

Wood. Speak out freely, you can tell me nothing

3   worfe

worfe than I imagine; you won't fhock me in the
leaft; not at all.

Jac. Well; there aw ware pleaying on that there
mufic-thing like a coffin, and madam ware a zinging
to un like any black-bird.

Wood. A mufic-mafter---Is that all, booby? (*pufhes
him down.*)

Jac. Yes; but t'other, zur---

Wood. Aye, I had forgot;---what of him, good
Jacob? what of him?

Jac. I ware never caall'd up while aw fteay'd; zo
(I can't but zeay, I had a curofity to knaw what
brought he here) one deay I peap'd thro' the keay-
hole, and zeed un---(*titters*)---I fhall never forget.

Wood. Tell me what this inftant, or I fhall burft
with rage and fufpenfe.

Jac. Screaping on a little viddle, no bigger than
my hand; while madam ware a huolding out her quoats,
and dancing all round the room zoa---(*mimicks the
minuet aukwardly.*)

Wood. Why, I believe the impudent bumpkin dares
to jeft with my mifery! and yet I have no other ave-
nue: for the reft, I fear, are knaves, and he feems only
a fool---and are thefe all that came, Jacob?

Jac. Noa, there were one moare, zur; a leetle
mon in a black quoat,---but he only com'd now and
tan.

Wood. A difguife, no doubt? Yes, yes, they were
artful enough.

Jac. And zoa, ater he had done wi' my Leady,
aw did fhut his felf up wi' Bridget; and zoa I axed

                    I   her

her all about un, and zhe zaid as how aw com'd to teach madam to turn themmin great round balls all blue, and red, and yellow, that do ftand by the books, and learned fhe to wroite.

Wood. Yes, yes, Mrs. Bridget was in all her fecrets, I don't doubt. If that fellow in black comes here again, keep him, if you value your life; and fend for me. I know not what to do or think, and muft renew my fearch, tho' hopelefs of fuccefs.   [*Exit.*

Jacob *alone.*

Jac. Dang it! but he's in a defperate teaking!--- Rabbit me, but I ware muortally afeard aw un too, for aw flourifh'd his zword as yeazy as I could a cudgel:---I do think conj'urer might as well ha tuold me madam would ha' run away, while aw ware about it, and then I moight ha' run away furft.   [*Exit.*

Enter Grey.

Grey. At length I have gaincd entrance into this houfe of fhame, which now, alas! contains my darling Cecilia,---plung'd in vice, and loft to every fentiment, I fpent fo many anxious years in implanting. This does not feem to be the abode of pleafure, nor have I met a fingle being.

Wood,

Woodville *entering behind, fees* Grey, *and drawing his sword, flies at and feizes him.*

Wood. Ha! a man! and in black, as Jacob faid! Villain, this moment is your laft.

Grey. (*turning fuddenly upon him*) Yes, young feducer, add to the daughter's ruin the father's murder! Stab my heart, as you already have my happinefs.

Wood. Alas, was *this* her vifitor? I dare not fpeak to him!

Grey. Embofomed by affluence, exalted by title, peace ftill fhall be far from thy heart; for thou, with the worft kind of avarice, haft by fpecious pretences wrefted from poverty its laft dear poffeffion,---virtue...

Wood. Pierced to the foul, as I am by your reproaches, I dare appeal to Cecilia herfelf for a teftimony of my contrition! How fhall I convince you?

Grey. Hardly by a life of repentance. But I debafe myfelf to exchange a word with you. Give me back my Cecilia!---Ruin'd as fhe is, I yet would recover her :---give her back then to a father you firft taught her to fear, and an habitation, too humble for any but the good to be happy in.

Wood. Alas, Sir! can you trifle with my mifery? do *you* give her back to the wretch who cannot furvive her lofs!---let me owe her hand to your bounty, tho' her heart to her own!---did you know what this elopement of her's has coft me---

Grey. Oh, moft accomplifh'd villain!---but think not to dupe *me* too.

Wood.

Wood. Who but you can have robb'd me of her since morning?

Grey. Shallow artifice!

Wood. Hear me, Sir! and even believe me, when I solemnly swear I have deeply repented my crime, and offer'd her all the reparation in my power;---but, since then----

Grey. What since then?

Wood. Either by your means, or some other, she has fled!

Grey. Impossible.

Wood. Tis too true, by heav'n!

Grey. Perhaps, while you are thus ingeniously deluding me, she *indeed* flies----Study some other deception, while I examine the whole house, for nothing else can convince me.   [*Exit.*

Woodville *alone.*

Surely this injur'd venerable man was sent by heav'n to complete my misfortunes!---my passions subside, but only into a vague horror and despondency, even more dreadful:---if with rash hand she has shorten'd her days, what remain of mine will be, indeed, all her father predicts! (*walking by the toilette*) ha, a letter!

Re-enter Grey.

Grey. A total loneliness in the house!

Wood. Now, sir, be convinc'd;---I have just found a letter from her.

Grey.

Grey. This cannot be the invention of a moment:
----let me read it---it is, indeed, her hand. (*Opens and reads it*)

" Receive this as my laft farewell.——Providence
" has unexpectedly fent me a friend, whofe protection
" I dare accept; and time may perhaps fubdue a paffion,
" which feems interwoven with my being.——Forget
" me, I intreat; and feek that happinefs with another,
" I can never hope to beftow or partake.——Confoled
" only by reflecting, that the grief, my error occafions,
" is inferior to that I fhould have felt, had I, by an
" ungenerous ufe of my power, made you, in turn,
" my victim.——Once more, adieu !——all fearch
" will certainly be fruitlefs."

   P. S. " In the cabinet you will find your valu-
    " able prefents; and the key is in a dreffing-
    " box."

(Woodville *fnatches the letter and burfts into tears*)
Grey. Cecilia ! I may fay, with tears of joy, thou
art, indeed, *my* daughter ! more dear (if poffible) than
ever ! a daughter monarchs might contend for, though
thy weak father abjures thee !——may the friend you
have found have a heart but like your own ! for you,
young man !—but I leave you to your anguifh ; the lofs
of *fuch* a woman is a fufficient punifhment.

Wood. Stay, fir ! (*rifes*) by your holy profeffion, I
conjure you, ftay !---plunge me not into total defpair !
---though without a clue to her afylum, I would fain
believe my heart will lead me to it; and let me then
hope you will beftow her on me ?

          Grey.

Grey. There is a fomething in your manner, young gentleman, that affects me;----I have been young, wild, and extravagant myself; and what is more ftrange, have not forgot I was fo: my own experience proves reformation poffible: act up to her and atone your error.

Wood. I will endeavour it, fir! and, oh could thofe who yet but waver, know what has paffed in my heart, during the laft hour, who would dare to deviate?   [*Exeunt.*

END OF THE THIRD ACT.

ACT IV.

SCENE, Cecilia's *House.*

Bridget dressed in Cecilia's *Clothes, mixed with every thing vulgar and tawdry.*

Brid. SO,---I am ready against our gentleman comes.---Deuce on him to run away last night, the moment I was dreft---and with an inferial fellow too! ---Lard, how can people of quality demean themfelves by keeping company with inferials!---however, one thing I am fure of, he's too much on the fidgets to ftay long away from our houfe; and in the mean while, I can entertain myfelf extremely well. (*Sits down to the toilette*)

Jac. (*Without*) I tell ye, my leady's not at huome.

Gov. I tell *you,* I won't take your word for it ;--- fo come, my Lord, and fee.

Brid. Heyday, my Lord !------what's the news now, I wonder?

Enter Lord Glenmore *and the* Governor; *both ſtop ſhort.*

Gov. Oh, I thought madam had learnt enough of the ton to lye by proxy.

Brid.

Brid. Dear heart!---I am all of a twitteration!---who can thefe be?---that's my Lord, for certain!

L. Glen. The vulgarity of the wench is aftonifhing!

Gov. ---Um---why, a little gawky, or fo,----there's no denying it.---(*afide*) Here's a pretty difcovery, now, after all my projects!---thank fortune, the fecret is yet my own though.

L. Glen. (*Advancing to her*) I ought to beg your excufe, madam, for fo abrupt an intrufion; but the opportunity and fo fair a temptation will, I flatter myfelf, be a fufficient apology.

Brid. (*afide*) He takes me for my lady, that's a fure thing!---oh, this is charming!---you need not make no 'pology's, my Lord;---inferials never knows how to fufpect people of quality; but I underftands good breeding better.

L. Glen. (*afide*) Why, what a Barn-door Mawkin it is! your politenefs, madam, can only be equalled by your beauty.

Brid. Dear heart, my Lord, you flatter me!------won't you pleafe to fit? (*waits affectedly 'till they confent to feat themfelves*)

L. Glen. (*to the* Governor) Surely by ufing my title, fhe knows me.

Gov. Zounds, I have a great mind to make her know *me*;---od, I fhall never be able to contain.

L. Glen. I was afraid, madam, I fhould prove an unwelcome gueft;---but beauty like yours---

Brid. Does your Lordfhip think I fo very handfome,

some then?---Lord, how lucky was my dreffing my-felf!

L. Glen. (*Afide*) Affected ideot! I was afraid, madam, too of meeting Woodville here---(*afide*) I know not what to fay to her.

Brid. He has not been here this morning; but, if he had, he knows better than to ax ater my company, I do affure you, my---Lordfhip.

L. Glen. I have been told he intends marrying you; what a pity to monopolize fuch merit!

Brid. If he has any fuch kind intention, 'tis more than I knows of, I affure you.

L. Glen. His keeping that wife refolution from you, is fome little comfort, however.

Brid. But, I promife ye, I fhall make a rare perfon of quality; for I loves cards, coaches, dancing, and drefs, to my very heart;---nothing in the world better--- but blindman's-buff. I had fome thoughts of taking a trip to Sadler's Wells or Fox Hall, but they don't begin 'till five o'clock.

Gov. (*Afide*) Ha! ha! tho' fhe can hardly fpell out the Ten Commandments, fhe could break every one with as much eafe and impudence, as if fhe had been bred in the circle of St. James's.

L. Glen. But, madam, you know, allowing Wood-ville willing to marry you, it is not in his power while his father lives, without forfeiting his fortune, the value of which you doubtlefs underftand?

Brid. Oh yes, yes, for fartain, my Lord.

L. Glen. Who knows too, how far an incenfed pa-rent may carry his refentment! he might find means to entrap and punifh you.

K   *Brid.*

Brid. Ha, ha, ha!---he entrap me!---that *would be* a good jeft!---no, no, I have more of the lady of quality than to be fo eafily caught.

Gov. (*mimicking her*) He, he, he! that is the only particular in which you have nothing at all of the lady of quality.

L. Glen. With me you may fhare a higher rank and larger fortune without thofe fears---*I* am of an age---

Brid. Yes, one may fee that without being a conjuror---why, will you marry me, my Lord?

L. Glen. Convince me that you don't love this Woodville, and I know not how far my paffion may carry me.

Brid. Love him? do you think I knows no more of high life than that comes to? To be fure, he is a fweet pretty man, and all that;---but, as to love, I loves nobody half fo well as myfelf.

L. Glen. Upon my foul, I believe you; and wifh he had the whole benefit of the declaration: [*To the Gover-nor*] her ingratitude is as fhocking as her ignorance, and Bridewell too gentle a punifhment.

Gov. Then build a bridewell large enough to contain the whole fex; for the only difference between her and the reft is,---this Country Mawkin *tells* what the Town-bred Miffes *conceal*.

L. Glen. Why, Governor, you are as tefty as if you had the care of *her* education.

Gov. I the care?---zounds, what I fay is merely from friendfhip to your Lordfhip.---I hate to fee you deceive yourfelf.---(*afide*) Surely he can never fufpect! {Bridget *is employed in cramming trinkets from the dref-fing-table into her pockets.)*

4

Brid.

Brid. Now I am ready to go, my Lord.

L. Glen. Reflect, madam! it would hurt me to have you say I deceiv'd you---if you should repent---I am much afraid you will.

Brid. What, when I am a lady? Oh, I'll venture that, and attend you.

Gov. (*roughly snatching her other hand*) To where you little dream of, you vain, affected, presuming, *ignorant baggage!*

Brid. Hey-day!---my Lord?

L. Glen. Appeal not to me, base woman!---know I am the father of that poor Dupe, Woodville:

Brid. Dear heart! be ye indeed? What will become of me then?

L. Glen. And, as a moderate punishment for your hypocrisy, ambition, and ingratitude, sentence you to be shut up for life in a monastery.

Brid. O Lord! among monsters?

Gov. No, Ignoramus!---no; among nuns: tho' *they* are but monsters in human nature either.

Brid. What, where they'll cut off my hair, and make me wear sackcloth next to my skin?

Gov. Yes, if they leave you any skin at all.

Brid. Oh dear, dear, dear! (*sobs and groans*) upon my bended knees, I do beg you won't send me there! ---why I shall go mallancholly-- I shall make away with myself for certain; and my ghost will appear to you all in white.

Gov. All in black, I rather think; for the devil a speck of white is there in your whole composition.

L. Glen.

L. Glen.   Your conduct, wretch! juftifies a feverer fentence--- to feduce him from his duty, was crime enough.

Brid.   Who, I feduce him? I did not, my Lord--- indeed I did not.

L. Glen.   Have you not own'd---

Brid.   No, indeed, no; that I wifh'd to take my Lady's place, I believe I did own:---

Gov.   Ha, ha, ha! very prettily devis'd, faith, for a young beginner!---come, come, (*chucking her under the chin*) we muft give you credit for this, Mifs---*your Lady?* ha, ha,---ha!

L. Glen.   Shallow fubterfuge!

Enter Vane *and the flaves.*

Vane, is all ready?---feize this woman, and obferve my orders!

Brid.   Ah dear heart! I fhall die away if the blacks do but touch me---indeed you do miftake!---I be no lady---I be only Bridget.

Gov.   I would give ten thoufand pounds that you *were* only Bridget, you artful pufs!---Zounds, tho' I could one moment ftrangle the pug's face in her own necklace, yet the next I can hardly prevail on myfelf to punifh her---what the devil had I *now* to do in England? or what the devil had I *ever* to do in Wales?--- Phew! I could dethrone fifty Nabobs without half the fatigue and anxiety of this moment.---Take her away, however! and let us try how Mifs likes riding out in her *own coach.*

[Vane *and the Slaves feize her;* fhe fcreams out *and catches* Lord Glenmore's *coat, falling on her knees.*---Jacob *enters, her back to him.*

Jac.

Jac. Why, what a dickens be ye all at here?---
Zoa, what's my Leady there?

L. Glen. See there now,---Oh the artful Jezebel!

Brid. Oh, Jacob! Why don't ye fee I am Bridget?---Pray fatisfy my Lord here.

Jac. Why, be ye Bridget?---Never truft me
elfe!

Gov. Here a fool of t'other fex now, can hardly
take a hint though fo plainly given him!---Thanks
to the natural difference, for art is nature in woman.
---(*L. Glen. draws him afide*)

Jac. Auh Bridget, Bridget! Where didft thee
get thee fum foine claws?---Noa, noa, as theeft
brew'd, thee meayft beake.

Brid. Oh, do ye take pity on me!---Why they
be going to carry me to fome outlandifh place, and
make a nunnery of me!

Jac. A nunnery? what's that? any thing Chriftin?
well, if I do fpake to um, will ye hae me?

Brid. Oh, yes, yes, yes!

L. Glen. Brother! I fhall leave you to the com-
pletion of this affair; I am fick to the foul of the
gawky---

Gov. Yes, yes; I don't doubt it,---I don't
doubt it,

L. Glen. (*To Vane.*) Convey her to my houfe, and
lock her up in one of the lofts over the ftables;---go
the backway, and even the family need know nothing
of the matter. The Chaplain will provide a licence,
and be ready---Courage, my lad, and depend upon
my gratitude! [*Exit.*

Gov.

Gov. Will you take her, or no?---I shall never
be able to stifle my agitation; and burst with rage if
I shew it.---

Jac. Why, zure, zure, ye won't carr' away our
Bridget?

Vane. Ha, ha, ha!

Gov. Oh, she *has* beat her meaning into thy
thick scull at last?--Pr'ythee, keep thy block-*head* out
of my way, if thou mean'st to keep it on thy own
shoulders.

Jac. Why, be ye in arnest then? dear heart alive!
why this is cousin Bridget!

Brid. Only send for Mr. Woodville.

Gov. Prettily devis'd again! ha, ha, ha! dost
think, my little dear! we have lived three times as
long. as your Ladyship to learn a quarter as much?---
Send for Mr. Woodville, hey?---No, no; you won't
find us quite so simple.

Jac. Oh doan't ye, doan't ye, carr' off zhe, or if
ye wull, do pray take I.

Vane. Yes, you would be a choice piece of lum-
ber truly.

Gov. Drag her away this moment.

Brid. Oh dear, oh dear! to be hanged at last for
another's crime is all that vexes me.

[*They carry her off*, Governor *follows.*

SCENE, *Miss* Mortimer's *Apartment.*

Cecilia *enters, and sits down to embroidery.*

How fond, how weak, how ungrateful, are our
hearts!---mine still will presumptuously fancy this
house its home, and ally itself to ev'ry one to whom
Woodville is dear.

Lord

Lord Glenmore *enters*.

Cec. Oh heaven's, my Lord !---how unlucky !---
if I go, he may find the Captain with Mifs Mortimer.

L. Glen. You fee, madam, you have only to retire
to engage us to purfue you, even to rudenefs.----But, tell
me, can it be your own choice to punifh us fo far as to
prefer folitude to our fociety ?

Cec. I know myfelf too well, my Lord, to receive
diftinctions of which I am unworthy ;---yet think not,
therefore, I fail in refpect.

L. Glen. But, is that charming bofom fufceptible of
nothing beyond refpect ? why is it capable of infpiring
a paffion it cannot participate ?

Cec. Your goodnefs, my Lord---my profound vene-
ration, will always attend you---but, the more gene-
neroufly you are inclined to forget what is due to yourfelf, the more ftrongly it is impreffed on my memory.

L. Glen. Were what you fay true, the bounties of
nature atone amply to you for the parfimony of fortune;
nor would your want of every other advantage leffen
your merit, or my fenfe of it.

Cec. (*afide*) Had he thought thus a few months fince,
how happy had I now been !---Your approbation at
once flatters and ferves me, by juftifying Mifs Mortimer's protection of me.

L. Glen. Her partiality for you, does her more honour than it can ever do you advantage. But, you
muft tell me, how fhe gain'd firft the happinefs of
knowing you ?

Cec.

Cec. My---my Lord, by a misfortune fo touching---

L. Glen. Nay, I would not diftrefs you neither; yet, I own, madam, I wifh to make a propofal worth a ferious anfwer; but ought firft to know, why you affect a myftery? Tell me then, my dear, ev'ry incident of your life, and I will raife you to a title, I may without vanity fay, many have afpired to!

Cec. You opprefs my very foul, my Lord! But, alas! unconquerable obftacles deprive me for ever of that title. Neither *would* I obtain it by alienating fuch a fon from fuch a father.

L. Glen. Put him entirely out of the queftion; the meannefs of his conduct acquits me to myfelf. Do you know, madam, he has refolved to marry a creature of low birth, illiterate, vulgar, and impudent? and, to complete her perfections, fhe has been *his* miftrefs at leaft.

Cec. Surely he knows, and purpofely fhocks me thus. (*Afide.*)

L. Glen. But your integrity doesn't render you lefs amiable in my eyes; it greatly enhances every other merit. As to his wretch, I have her in my power, and fhall make her dearly repent.

Cec. Then I am loft indeed! (*afide*) You have, my Lord; tho' I know not how, difcovered.----(*Rifes in confufion.*)

L. Glen. (*rifes, taking fnuff, without looking at her*) Oh, nothing more eafy, madam; I had him carefully traced to her houfe; and, during his abfence, took fervants and forced her away.

Cec. (*afide*) That, however, cannot be me; every word feems to add to a myftery I dare not enquire into.

L. Glen.

L. Glen. But why wafte one precious moment on fuch an animal? what are thefe unconquerable obfta- cles?

Cec. Spare me, my Lord; your indulgence induces me to try again to foften your refolutions refpecting your fon: deprived of the weak, the guilty, the miferable wretch you juftly condemn, a little time will (no doubt) incline him to his duty. I fhould have your pardon to folicit, my Lord, but that your own opennefs autho- rizes mine.

L. Glen. But, can you, who fo powerfully plead the caufe of another, be deaf to the fighs of a man who adores you? who offers you a rank---

Cec. Be fatisfied, my Lord, with knowing I have all that efteem your merit claims; which influences *me* beyond every cafual advantage.

L. Glen. But, madam---

Cec. Alas! my Lord!---*(burfts into tears afide)*--- Be filent, if poffible, both pride and virtue. I have de- ferved, and will fubmit to it---yet furely the bitternefs of this moment expiates all paft offences. [*Exit.*

L. Glen. Amiable creature! what an amazing ele- gance of mind and perfon! Tears were her only an- fwers to my queftions, and blufhes to my looks: yet thefe only heighten a curiofity they have foftened into love. [*Exit.*

Woodville's *Apartment.*

Woodville *alone.*

Wood. No intelligence of my Cecilia yet!---were I only affured of her fafety, it would be fome confola- tion.

L. *Enter*

Enter Jacob.

Jac. Zur, Zur !---I do maeke fo bowld as tò ax to fpake to yóu.

Wood. Jacob! my honeſt fellow, the very fight of thee revives my hopes, and fets my heart in motion! ---well, what's the news?

Jac. Zurprizing news indeed, zur !---Loord, I thought I ſhould never meat wi'ye ;---I com'd to your lodgings twice, and ye warn't up.

Wood. Up ! 'ſdeath, you ignorant booby ! why did'nt you order them to rouſe me that moment?

Jac. Loord, zur ! why your gentleman (as they do caal un) were fo terrable foine, I were afeard of affronting un !

Wood. Plague on the ſtupidity of both, ſay I !--- But what's all this to the purpofe? the news? tho news?

Jac. Las-a-deazy ! mourtal bad news, indeed !---

Wood. You tedious blockhead! is your lady return'd?

Jac. Noa, Zur. (*Shaking his head very mourn-fully.*)

Wood. (*afide*) The horrid forebodings of my heart recur; yet, furely ſhe could not be fo defperate !--- ſhocking as the fufpenfe is, I more dread the certainty. ---Speak, however, my good fellow ! (*Jacob wipes his eyes*)---I ſhall ever value your fenfibility.---Tell me then the fimple truth, whatever it may be?---

Jac. I wull, Zur, I wull.---There has com'd two foine gentlemen, wi zwords by their zides, juſt for all the world like yourn.

                                        Wood.

Wood. Well, and what did thefe gentlemen fay?

Jac. Why, they went up ftears, willy nilly, and carr'd off------ our Bridget. *(Burfts out a crying.)*

Wood. You impudent, ignorant clown! I'll give you caufe for your tears. *(Shakes him.)*

Jac. Loord! Loord!---do ye ha a little Chriftin commiferation---well, if I ever do coume nigh ye again, I do wifh ye may break every buone in my zkin.

Wood. *(Walking about in a rage)* To infult me with your own paltry love affairs! thefe great and mighty gentlemen were only conftables I dare fwear, and your fears converted their ftaves to fwords.

Jac. Ay, but that an't the worft neither. I do verily think my turn wull cuome next;---can't zleep in my bed for thinking on't, nor enjoy a meal's meat:---zo, except you do bring your zword, and coume and live in our houze, I wull guo out on't, that's a zure thing; for I had rather fceare craws at a graat a deay all my loife long, than bide there to be fo terrified.

Wood. Sceare craws truly? why the craws will fceare you, ye hen-hearted puppy!---there, teake that, *(gives him money),* and guo huome, or to the devil, fo you never fall in my way again.

Jac. Zome faulk that I do knaw wull zee the black gentleman firft, 'tis my belief---zoa I had beft keep out o' his woiy too.

Enter Harcourt.

Har. Woodville, what's the matter? why you will raife the neighbourhood.

Jacob

Jacob *returns.*

Jac. Here's a peaper housemaid do zend you, wi'
her humble duty; but, if zo be it do put ye in another desperate teaking, I do huope ye wull zend for
zhe to beat, and not I.---Loord! Loord! what wull
becuome of me in this woide world of London!

[*Exit Jacob.*

Har. Ha! ha! ha! he is a choice fellow!

Wood. A heart oppressed with its own feelings,
fears ev'ry thing. I have hardly courage to open a
letter without an address.

Har. Come, come, give it me then. Hey, what?
confusion!---was ever any thing so unlucky? (*at-
tempts to tear it.*)

Wood. (*snatches it from him*) Ha! it is important
then?

Har. Why will you invent torments for yourself?
(*aside*)---My own letter by ev'ry thing careless---
here's a stroke----

Wood. (*reads in a broken voice and manner*) "Wood-
"ville on the brink of marriage---you will be disen-
"gaged---a nobleman---(damnation!)---heart and
"fortune at her feet"---(I'll let his soul out there)
hell and furies!---but I will find him, if money
---never will I close my eyes till---Oh Cecilia---
(*throws himself into a seat.*)

Har. This is the most unforeseen---I know not
what to say to him---prythee, Woodville! do not sa-
crifice so many reasonable presumptions in her favour,
to a paper that may be a forgery, for aught you know!

Wood.

Wood. Oh Charles! that I could think fo!---but I have feen the villain's execrable hand fomewhere! Did you never fee the hand?

Har. Um---I can't but own I have,---what the devil fhall I fay to him---(*Afide.*)

Enter the Governor.

Gov. Woodville, my dear boy! I am come to have a little talk with thee.---Charles! don't run away!---you are in all your coufin's fecrets.

Wood. What fhould poffefs this tirefome mortal to come here?---I fhould have waited on *you*, in half an hour, Sir.

Gov. Ay, and that's what I wanted to avoid:--- The more I talk to your father, Frank, the more I find him fixed on the match with his Mifs Mortimer! Nay, he tells me, he will have you married this very day.

Wood. That's mighty probable in the humour I am in.

Gov. Ah, Frank! the girl I offer thee---

Wood. Is no more agreeable to me than her you defpife.

Gov. How do you know that, peppercorn?---how do you know that?---od, I could tell you---

Wood. And, to tell you my full mind, Sir, I had rather make myfelf miferable to gratify my father, than any other man.

Gov. Od! thou art fo obftinate, boy, I can't help loving thee.---(*Afide*) I don't fee why I am obliged to know his Mifs is my daughter—I have a great mind to own what we have done with her; and, if he will marry, e'en take care nobody hinders him! then, trump up a farce about forgiving them;—and yet, it goes againft my confcience to punifh the puppy for life, though he has punifhed me pretty fufficiently, by the Lord Harry.

Har. I don't like this affair at all, and tremble for my Sophia, when I fee this odd foul fo inveterate againft her.

Gov. (*to Woodville*) Well, my lad! do you know I am as deep in all your fecrets as your favourite valet de chambre?

Wood. I don't underftand you, Sir.

Gov. Pho, pho, pho! keep that face till I fhew thee one as folemn as my Lord's. Why fhould not you pleafe yourfelf, and marry *your* Mifs, inftead of your father's?

Both. Aftonifhing!

Gov. Od, if you turn out the honeft fellow I take you for, I know a pretty round fum, an onion and a black coat may one day or other entitle you to; fo never mind Lord Gravity's refentment.

Wood. I act from better motives, Sir, and were unworthy your wealth could it tempt me to difobey the beft of fathers.

Gov. (*paffionately*) Why then, marry Mifs Morti-mer, and oblige him: take a back feat in your own coach, get a family of pale-faced brats, born with of-trich feathers on their heads; and hate away a long life with all due decorum!——Zounds, here's a fellow

more

more whimfical than---even myfelf.---Yefterday you
would have the pufs fpite of every body; but, you no
fooner find it in your power to oblige your beft friend,
by humouring your inclinations, than, lo! you are taken with a moft violent fit of duty and fubmiffion!---
Od, you don't know what you have loft by it!---
but, fince you are bent on croffing me, I'll crofs you,
and once for all too---My fecret fhall henceforth be
as impenetrable as the philofopher's ftone.---Ay, ftare
as you pleafe, I'll give you more years than you have
yet feen days to guefs it in.   [*Exit.*

Har. What this uncle of ours can mean is quite
beyond my guefs!

Wood. What fignifies feeking to expound by reafon, actions in which it had no fhare?---his brain is
indubitably touched! but Cecilia lies heavy on my
heart, and excludes ev'ry other thought.

Har. Time may explain the fecret of that letter,
which, I will lay my life, fhe defpifes:---a woman
who did not, would have kept it from your hands.

Wood. That's true, indeed!--- if I wrong her, and
this was but an infult,---there is a noble fincerity in
her own letter which fets fufpicion at defiance.---If
he ftumbled on one word of truth during this vifit,
the crifis of my fate approaches.---Oh, wherever
thou art, if the exalted being I will ftill hope my
Cecilia, thou fhalt know I have at leaft deferv'd
thee!   [*Exeunt.*

END OF THE FOURTH ACT.

A C T

ACT V.

SCENE, *A mean Room; Boots, Bridles, &c. hang-ing all round.*

Bridget *fitting very mournfully, her fine Clothes in great Diforder;---a Table by her, with a fmall Roll, a Glafs of Water, an old dog's-ear'd Book, and a Bit of Looking-glafs.*

Brid. DEAR heart! dear heart! what a miferable time have I pafs'd! and, where I be to pafs my whole life, my Lord here only knows!---I have' not much ftomach indeed; neither have I much breakfaft. (*Eats a bit of bread and burfts into tears.*)

Enter the Governor.

Gov. Had I more fins to anfwer for than a college of Jefuits, I furely expiate them all, by going through a purgatory in this life beyond what they have in-vented for the other.---This vulgar Maux of mine haunts my imagination, in every fhape but that I hoped to fee her in; I dare hardly truft myfelf to fpeak to her! ---od, I would not have the extirpation of the whole female fex depend upon my cafting-vote while I am in this humour.

Brid.

Brid. Mercy on me! here's that crofs old gentleman again! what will become of me?---do, pray,
ftrange fir!· be fo generous, as to tell me what is next
to be done with me?

Gov. Why, juft whatever I pleafe, you audacious
baggage!---(*Afide*) od, now I think on't, I have a
great mind to try a few foft words, and dive into all
the fecrets of the little ignoramus.---Come, fuppofe I
had a mind to grant you your freedom, how would
you requite me?

Brid. Dear heart! why I'd love you for ever and
ever.

Gov. 'dzounds, that's a favor I could very readily
difpenfe with;---and yet 'tis natural to the poor
wench:---Ah! if thou had'ft been a good girl, thou
had'ft been a happy one.--Hark'ye, mifs! confefs all
your fins, that's the only way to efcape, I promife
you! and, if you conceal the leaft, I'll--------do, I
don't know what I'll do to you.

Brid. I will; I will, fir, indeed, as I hope to be
married.

Gov. Married, you flut! bad as that is, it's too
good for you:---come, tell me all your adventurers?
---defcribe the behaviour of the young villain who feduced you;---where did you fee him firft?

Brid. Ugh, ugh,---At church, fir.

Gov. At church, quotha?---a pretty place to com-
mence an intrigue in!---and how long was it before you
came to this admirable agreement?

Brid. Umh?---why--Sunday was Midfummer-eve,
---and Sunday ater was madam's wedding-day,---and
Monday was our fair, and---

M

Gov.

Gov. Oh, curfe your long hiſtories!---and, what then ſaid Woodville?

Brid. Oh Lord, nothing at all---why, it warn't he.---

Gov. No!---*(ready to burſt with paſſion)* Who, who, who? tell me that, and quite diſtract me!

Brid. Timothy Hobbs, Squire's gardener.

Gov. an abſolute clown--- *(walks about half groaning with rage and diſappointment)* who, oh! who would be a father?--I could laugh,---cry,---die,---with ſhame and anger!---ſince the man, who corrupted, left her only one virtue, would he had deprived her of that too!---oh, that ſhe had but ſkill enough to lye well!

Brid. Whether I can or no, I'll never ſpeak truth again, that's a ſure thing!---what do I get by it, or any poor ſouls of the female kind?

Gov. I am incapable of thinking;---ev'ry plan, ev'ry reſource thus overturn'd;---I muſt be wiſer than all the world?---This fool's head of mine muſt take to teaching truly! as if I could eradicate the ſtamp of nature, or regulate the ſenſes, by any thing but reaſon---don't pipe, baggage! to me;---you all can do that, when too late:---when I have conſidered whether I ſhall hang myſelf or not, I'll let you know whether I ſhall tuck you up along with me, you little wretch, you!   *Exit.*

Bridget *alone.*

Brid. Well, ſure I have at laſt gueſs'd where I am ſhut up!---it muſt be Bedlam; for the old gentleman is out of his mind, that's a ſure thing!   *Enter*

Enter Vane.

Van. Ha, ha, ha! my future father-in-law seems to have got a quietus of my intended; and, faith, so wou'd any man who was not in love with a certain forty thousand;---to be sure, in plain English, she is a glorious mawkin!---*(to her)*---well, madam, how are you pleas'd with your present mode of living?

Brid. Living, do you call it?---I think, 'tis only starving.---Why, I shall eat my way through the walls very shortly.

Van. Faith, Miss, they use you but so so, that's the truth on't; and I must repeat, even to your face, what I said to my Lord, that your youth, beauty and accomplishments, deserve a better fate.

Brid. Dear heart! Bedlam, did I say, I was in! why, I never knew a more sensibler, genteeler prettier sort of a man in my life. *(aside)*---I am sure, Sir, if I was to study seven years, I shou'd never know what I have done to discommode them, not I.

Van. Oh Lard, my dear! only what is done ev'ry day by half your sex without punishment---however, you are to suffer for all, it seems?---you see your fare for life!--- a dungeon, coarse rags, and the same handsome allowance of bread and water twice a day.

Brid. Oh, dear me!---why I shall be an otomy in a week!

Van. And an old black to guard you, more sulky and hideous, than those in the Arabian Night's Entertainments,

M 2   *Brid,*

Brid. Why, fure they will let you come and fee me, Sir? I fhall certainly fwound away, every time I look at that nafty old black.

Van. This is the laft time your dungeon (which your prefence renders a palace to me) will ever be open to one vifitor—unlefs---unlefs---I cou'd contrive--- but no, it would be my ruin: yet who woud'nt venture fomething for fuch a charming creature? you could endear even ruin.----Tell me, then, what reward you would beftow on a man who ventur'd all to give you freedom?

Brid. Nay, I don't know; you're fuch a dear fweet foul, I fhan't ftand with you for a trifle.

Van. Ahey! Mifs will be as much too comply- ing in a minute.----Well, then, my dear! I muft marry you, or you will ftill be in the power of your enemies.

Brid. Hey?---what? do I hear rightly? marry me? ---(*afide*)---why, this will be the luckieft day's work I ever did !---nay, Sir, if you fhould be fo generous, I hope I fhall live to make you amends!

Van. (*afide*) The only amends you can make me, is by dying---and now, my dear! I will own to you, I have the licenfe in my pocket; and my Lord, as eager as myfelf.----Our chaplain will do us the favour with more expedition than he fays grace before meat !--- Well done, Vane! egad, thy lucky ftar predominates! ---(*Afide---takes her arm*)

Brid. Surely my locking up does end very comi- cal.   [*Exeunt arm in arm.*

SCENE.

A COMEDY.

SCENE,---*The drawing room.*

Mifs Mortimer *and Captain* Harcourt.

M. Mor. Woodville is now with his father, and both
in the decifive mood.----Oh, Charles! as the moment
approaches nearer, your influence becomes infenfibly
lefs powerful:---the frantic fits of the Governor; the
folemn abfurdity of my Lord---but, above all, the behaviour of Woodville, hurts and alarms me!---ftill
cautious not to offend his father, he has tried ev'ry
way to extort the refufal from me; but, by a pardon-
able equivocation, I left him hopelefs, and affured him I
fhould, to the utmoft of my power, obey my benefactor.----Why, why did you marry one, who could give
you nothing but her heart?

Har. I fhall not anfwer, till you can name me an
equivalent---truft to my management, my dear Sophia.---I ftill flatter myfelf, one ftorm will fettle the
tenor of our lives---if not; while acquitted to Heav'n,
the world, and ourfelves, we may ftruggle with fpirit
againft fortune; and fometimes owe our deareft enjoyments to her fluctuations.

M. Mor. By fentiments like thefe you won my
very foul; and to retain for ever a heart fo invaluable,
I have ventur'd the difpleafure of my benefactor: but
our hearts will not always follow the lead of our reafon, nor, when I confider the caufe, can I repent the
deviation of mine,

Har.

Har. Think, if you pity yourfelf, what you can give to Cecilia; and fortify her mind againft too ftrong a fenfe of her frailty. For my part, I muft watch whatever is going on.

M. Mor. So you leave me out of the plot?---well, if it ends happily, I fhall be contented; and, like the world, meafuring your merit by your fuccefs, will declare you a moft inimitable fchemer.---Adieu!

Har. Nay, ftay a moment!

M. Mor. Not for the world; for here comes your uncle, with a face more petrifying than Medufa's. [*Exit.*

Enter the Governor, *mufing.*

Gov. I have lived fifty eight years, five months, and certain odd days, to find out I am a fool at laft; but I will live as many more, before I add the difcovery that I am a knave too.

Har. What the devil can he be now hatching? ---mifchief, I fear?

Gov. Dear fortune! let me efcape this once undifcover'd, and I compound for all the reft.---Charles! the news of the houfe? for the politics of this family are employment for ev'ry individual in it.

Har. Bella, horrida bella, Sir!---my Lord is determined to bring his fon's duty to an immediate teft,---(*afide*) thanks to his friend's fchemes and his miftrefs's beauty.

Gov. What poor malicious wretches are we by nature!----Zounds, if I could not find in my heart to rejoice

rejoice at thinking every one here will be as mortified
and difappointed as a certain perfon that fhall be
namelefs.----So, fo; here they come, faith, to argue
the point in open court.

Enter Lord Glenmore *followed by* Woodville.

L. Glen. Without this proof of your obedience, all
you can urge, Sir, is ineffectual.

Wood. While obedience was poffible, I never fwerv'd,
my Lord ; but, when you command me to make myfelf wretched, a fuperior duty cancels that:——already
bound by a voluntary, an everlafting vow, I cannot break it without offending heav'n, nor keep it
without offending you.

Gov. (*afide*) What's this ? chop'd about again !

Wood. Did you once know the incomparable merits of my love, even your Lordfhip's prejudices muft
give way to your reafon.

L. Glen. Mere dotage.----Doesn't her conduct
equally evince her folly and depravity ?

Wood. Cover'd as I ought to be, with confufion
and remorfe ; I will own fhe was feduced and deceiv'd.

Gov. (*afide*) Ah, poor boy !---*one* of the two was
woefully deceiv'd fure enough.

L. Glen. Oh, your confcience may be very eafy on
that account ; it could not require much art to deceive
fuch an ideot.

Gov. No, no, my Lord ; why paint the devil blacker
than he is ? not an ideot neither.

Wood.

Wood. Sir, my father's freedom of speech I muſt endure ;—but yours---

Gov. You muſt endure too, young Sir, or I ſhall
bite my tongue off.

Wood. But, my Lord! that dear unhappy girl is
no longer a ſubjeƈt of debate,---ſhe evidently proves
her merit by her flight.

L. Glen. Would you make a virtue from not doing ill, when it is no longer in your power?---Wood-
ville! I was once weak enough to believe indulgence
the ſureſt way of obtaining your duty and eſteem.---
My eyes are at laſt opened,---Miſs Mortimer. is worthy a better huſband ; but you are her's or no ſon of
mine.---I ſolemnly promiſed this to her dying father,
and will acquit myſelf at all events.

Wood. Can you reſolve to ſacrifice me to a promiſe
made before we could judge of each other?---You
never felt, Sir, the compulſion you praƈtice ;---will you
diſſolve the firſt band of morality, and ſee your highly-
eſtimated title end in me ? for never will I on theſe
terms continue it.

L. Glen. I almoſt wiſh *I* never had continued it.--
(*Walks in anger.*) I am determined, Woodville! and
nothing but Miſs Mortimer's refuſal can break the
match.

Wood. I ſhall not put that in her power, my Lord:
Permit me to tell you, no ſon was ever more ſenſi-
ble of a father's kindneſs: but, if I can purchaſe its
continuance only with my honour and my happineſs,
it would be too dearly bought.

3

L. Glen.

L. Glen. 'Tis well, sir.——I have listened to you sufficiently. Now hear ME. Know, this worthless wretch, you prefer to your duty, is in my power; nay, in this house.

Har. (*aside*) The devil she is! how in the name of ill-luck should he find that out?---my fine scheme entirely blown up, by Jupiter!

Wood. Why play thus upon me, my Lord?---her letter---,

L. Glen. What, has she wrote to you?---that I was not aware of, nor indeed suspected she could write.

Gov. No, not so ignorant as that neither. I order'd she should write too!

L. Glen. You order'd she should write?---let me tell you, sir, it was wronging my confidence!

Gov. No, I did *not* order she should write;---I mean,---I mean,---zounds! I don't know what I mean!

Wood. So it seems, indeed, since hardly half an hour ago my uncle himself persuaded me to marry my love.

Gov. Here's a cursed affair now.

L. Glen. Can this be possible? Let me tell you, Governor, if presuming upon your wealth, you play a double part in my family---

Gov. Zounds! nobody knows his *own* part in your family, that I see! and this fellow, too, to teize me, whom I lov'd above all in it. Why, I spoke entirely from regard to him. If, since then I have discovered

N　　　　　　　a bumpkin

a bumpkin was beforehand with him in the poſſeſſion of his miſs---

Wood. If any one, beſide yourſelf, ſir, durſt tell ſuch a falſehood; it would coſt a life.

Gov. Yes; and, if any one beſide myſelf durſt tell me ſuch a truth, it would coſt a ſoul perhaps.

[*Exit.*

Har. This is more unintelligible than all the reſt.

L. Glen. To end theſe altercations;---upon your-ſelf, Woodville, ſhall depend the fortune of this wretch, to whom you have been ſo groſs a dupe as to juſtify the imputation of folly. Why, even without knowing me, ſhe ridiculed your paſſion, and offered to leave you.

Wood. Impoſſible!

L. Glen. Dare you diſbelieve me, ſir?---nay, ſhe ſhall be produced, and obliged to confeſs her arts;--- then bluſh and obey! Here, Vane! Governor, the keys! [*Exit.*

(Woodville *walks behind in great agitation.*

Har. Now could I find in my heart to make this ſtory into a ballad, as a warning to all meddling pup-pies; and then hang myſelf, that it may conclude with a grace. Zounds, he muſt be endued with ſu-pernatural intelligence. Juſt when I was ſaying a thouſand civil things to myſelf on my ſucceſs, to have my mine ſprung before my eyes by the enemy; and, inſtead of ſerving my friend and myſelf, become a meer tool to old Gravity's revenge! 'Pſhaw! how-ever, we muſt make the beſt of a bad matter.------ Woodville, what do'ſt mean to do, man?

Wood.

Wood.   Let them produce my Cecilia!---I will then feize, and protect her to the laft moment of my life.

Har.   And I will affift you to 'the laft moment of mine.

Wood.   My generous coufin! this is indeed friend-fhip.

Har.   Not fo very generous, if you knew all.

Re-enter Lord Glenmore *and the* Governor, *with* Bridget *holding a handkerchief to her eyes,* Vane *fol-lowing ;* Woodville *flies and clafps her in his arms ;* Harcourt *takes her hand.*

Wood. My love! my life!---do I once again be-hold thee?---fear nothing!---you here are fafe from all the world!---will you not blefs me with one look?

Brid. (*looking at him and* Harcourt *with ridiculous diftrefs*) Oh, dear me!

L. Glen.   I have put it out of your power to mar-ry, Sir, otherwife you may take her.

Wood.   'Take *her!*---what poor farce is this?

Har.   Hey-day! more incomprehenfibilities.

Van.   (*Afide*) Now for the eclairciffement---fince, if the Governor doesn't acknowledge her in his firft rage and confufion, I may never be able to make him!---I humbly hope, Mr. Woodville will pardon me, if, with her own confent and my Lord's, *I* this morning married this young lady.

Gov.   Zounds, you dog, what's that?---*you* mar-ried her!---why, how did you dare---and you

too,

too, my Lord!---what the devil, did you confent to this?

Vane. Believe me, fir, I didn't then know fhe was your daughter.

L. Glen. Daughter!

Gov. So, it's out, after all:---it's a lye, you dog! you *did* know fhe was my daughter;---you all knew it;---you all confpired to torment me!

All. Ha, ha, ha!

Gov. Ha, ha, ha! confound your mirth!---as if I had not plagues enough already.---And you have great reafon to grin too, my Lord, when you have thrown away my Gawky on your impudent valet.

L. Glen. Who could ever have dreamt of---ha, ha, ha---of finding *this* your little wonder of the country, brother?

Har. Nay, my Lord, fhe's the little wonder of the town, too.

All. Ha, ha, ha!

Gov. Mighty well,-----mighty well,----mighty well; pray, take your whole laugh out, good folks; fince this is, pofitively, the laft time of my entertaining you in this manner.---A cottage fhall henceforth be her portion, and a rope mine.

Brid. I you *are* my papa, I think you might give fome beter proof of your kindnefs;---but I fhan't ftir;---why, I married on purpofe that I might not care for you.

Gov. Why, thou eternal torment!---my original fin!---whofe firft fault was the greateft frailty of woman; and whofe fecond, her greateft folly! do'ft

thou,

thou, or the defigning knave who has entrapped thee merely for that purpofe, imagine my wealth fhall ever reward incontinence and ingratitude?---no; go knit ftockings to fome regiment were he is preferred to be drummer!---warm yourfelf when the fun fhines!---foak ev'ry hard-earned cruft in your own tears, and repent at leifure.   [*Exit in a rage.*

All. Ha, ha, ha!

L. Glen. *He* to ridicule my mode of education!---- but what is the meaning of all this?

Wood. Truly, my Lord, I believe it would be very hard to find any for either my uncle's words or actions.----I am equally at a lofs to guefs as to Bridget here.

Vane. Hey, what? Bridget, did you fay, fir? why you little ugly witch, are you really Bridget?

Brid. Why, I told ye fo all along; but you wou'dn't believe me.

All. Ha, ha, ha!

Brid. Oh dear heart!---I am now as much afeard of my new hufband as father.

L. Glen. For thee, wench----

Brid. (*pops upon her knees*) Oh, no more locking up, for goodnefs fake, my Lord---I be fick enough of paffing for a lady: but, if old Scratch ever puts fuch a trick again in my head, I hope---your Lordfhip will catch me! that's all.   :   . [*Exit.*

Vane. I fhall run diftracted! have I married an--- and all for nothing too?

L. Glen. A punifhment peculiarly juft, as it re-fults from abufing my confidence----Hence, wretch!

nor

nor ever, while you live, appear again in my prefence.   [*Exit* Vane, *looking furiously after* Bridget.

L. Glen. 'Tis time to return to ourfelves. We
fhall foon come to an eclairciffement, Woodville!---
Since *you* won't marry, I will.

Wood. My Lord!

L. Glen. And you fhall judge of my choice. [*Exit.*

Har. Now for it;---whatever devil diverts himfelf among us to-day, I fee he owes my fagacious
Lord here a grudge, as well as the reft; and I forefee
that his wife and the Governor's daughter will prove
equally entertaining.

Enter Lord Glenmore *leading* Cecilia, *followed by Mifs*
Mortimer.

L. Glen. This Lady, Sir, I have felected;---a
worthy choice.

Wood. I dream, furely!---that lady your choice?
---*yours!*

L. Glen. Ungrateful fon! had fuch been yours---

Wood. Why, this very Angel *is* mine, my Cecilia, my firft, my only love.

L. Glen. How!---

Cec. Yes, my Lord!---you now know the unhappy object at once of your refentment, contempt,
and admiration!---my own misfortunes I had learnt
to bear, but thofe of Woodville overpower me!---
I deliver myfelf up to your juftice; content to be
ev'ry way his victim, fo I am not his ruin.

L. Glen. But to find you in this houfe---

Cec.

Cec. Your generous nephew and the amiable Mifs Mortimer diftinguifh'd me with the only afylum could fhelter me from your fon !

L. Glen. They diftinguifhed *themfelves !*----Oh, Woodville ! did I think an hour ago I could be more angry with you ?---How durft you warp a mind fo noble ?

Wood. It is a crime my life cannot expiate,---yet, if the fincereft anguifh---

L. Glen. I have one act of juftice ftill in my power; ---my prejudice in favour of birth, and even a ftronger prejudice, is corrected by this lovely girl:---of her goodnefs of heart, and greatnefs of mind, I have had inconteftible proofs, and, if I thought you, Frank---

Cec. Yet, ftay, my Lord ! nor kill me with too much kindnefs.---Once your generofity might have made me happy, now only miferable.---My reafon, my pride, nay even my love, induces me to refufe as the only way to prove I deferve him !---he has taught me to know the world too late, nor will I retort on him the contempt I have incurr'd.---Mr. Woodville will tell you whether I have not folemnly vow'd---

Wood. Not to accept me without the confent of both fathers; and, if mine confents, what doubt---

Governor *without.*

Stop that old man ! ftop that mad parfon ! ftop him !

Grey.

Grey *without.*

Nothing shall stop me in pursuit of my---(*enters*)
Ha! she is---she is here indeed! providence has at
length directed me to her (*runs to* Cecilia)

Cec. My father! cover'd with shame let me sink before you.

L. Glen. and *Har.* Her father!

Enter Governor.

Grey. Rise, my glorious girl! rise purified and forgiven! rise to pity with me the weak minds that
know not all thy value, and venerate the noble ones
that do.

Gov. Hey! is it possible! Grey, is this my---

'*Gov.* Yes, Sir; this is your Cecilia, my Cecilia, the
object of your avowed rejection and contempt!

Gov. Rejection and contempt! stand out of the way
---let me embrace my daughter---let me take her once
more to my heart---(*runs and embraces her.*)

L. Glen. His daughter!

Gov. Yes, my friends, this is *really* my daughter---
my own Cecilia, as sure as I am an old fool after being
a young one, this good girl has a right to call me so by
the name of father.---Hasn't she, Grey?--why my Lord,
this is the very parson I told you of?---(*taking* Cecilia's
arm under his) and *now,* young Sir, what do you say to
your uncle's freaks?

Wood. Say, Sir? that had you ten thousand such I
would go through a patriarchal servitude, in hopes of
Cecilia's hand for my reward.

4   *Gov.*

Gov. And, had I ten millions of money, and this only girl, thou should'ft have her, and that, too, for thy noble freedom.----And what fays my Cecilia to her father's firft gift?

Cec. Aftonifhment and pleafure leave me hardly power to fay, that a difobedience to you, fir, would only double my fault: nor to worfhip that Heav'n, which has led me through fuch a trial, to fuch a reward!---take all I have left myfelf to give you, Woodville, in my hand---(*Woodville kiffes firft her band, and then herfelf.*)

Grey. Now, let me die, my darling child! fince I have feen thee, once more, innocent and happy.

Gov. And now, kifs me, my Cecilia!---kifs me! ---od, Mifs Mortimer fhall kifs me too, for loving my poor girl here!---kifs me, all of you, old and young! men, women and children!---od, I am fo overjoyed, I dread the confequences.------D'ye hear, there?--- fetch me a furgeon and a bottle of wine!------I muft both empty and fill my veins on this occafion------zooks I could find in my heart to frifk it merrily in defiance of the gout, and take that curfed vixen below, whoever fhe is, for my partner!

L. Glen. Methinks all feem rewarded, but my poor Sophia here? and her protection of Cecilia deferves the higheft recompence: but whenever, my dear, you can prefent me the hufband of your choice, I will prefent him with a fortune fit for my daughter.

Gov. Protect Cecilia! od! fhe is a good girl, and a charming girl, and I honour the very tip of her feathers now!---if fhe could but fancy our Charles,

O   I'd

I'd throw in something pretty on his side, I promise you.

Miss Mor. Frankness is the fashion.---What would you say, sir, and you, my Lord, if I *had* fancied your Charles so much, as to make him mine already ?

Gov. Hey-day! more discov'ries! how's this, boy?

Har. Even so, sir, indeed.

L. Glen. It completes my satisfaction.

Gov. Od, brother! who'd have thought you in the right all the while?---we'll never separate again, by the Lord Harry! but knock down our Welch friend's old house, and raise him one on the ruins, large enough to contain the whole family of us, where he shall reign sole sov'reign over all our future little Woodville's and Cecilias.

Cec. Oppressed with wonder, pleasure, gratitude, I must endeavour to forgive *myself*, when heav'n thus graciously proves its forgiveness, in allying me to ev'ry human being my heart distinguishes.

Grey. Yes, my Cecilia, you may believe him, who never gave you a bad lesson, that you are now most truly entitled to esteem; since it requires a far greater exertion to stop your course down the hill of vice, than to toil slowly up toward virtue.

THE END.

CPSIA information can be obtained
at www.ICGtesting.com
Printed in the USA
BVHW040859160223
658643BV00014B/310